"Family Types is a fascinating guide to your child's personality. It is clearly written, and easy to understand. You'll enjoy reading about the personality types, and figuring out what type your kids' are. I recommend this book to anyone who wants to use this unique and useful tool to help with parenting!"

~ **Jacqueline Green**
*Creator/Host of the Great Parenting Show
– The #1 Online Resource for Parenting World Wide*

"Selah Cambias makes it easy to see the patterns in your child's behavior—good and bad. She gives practical instructions about how to use the kids' different archetypes to recognize what's behind the actions and emotions, and shows how to prevent unwanted reactions. Better still, she shows how to use those traits to empower and support children to be the best they can be. Once you recognize the child's archetypes (and that's easy too) parenting becomes a true joy.

~ **Alenka Tercic**
www.sparklingkids.com

Who's in My House?

Warrior? Angel? Hermit? I had no idea these beings were all living in my house. But now that I do, the challenges of parenting my three children have gotten easier and the path clearer. Selah Cambias has given me a practical, intelligent framework for understanding my children better and for applying this to my daily life as a dad. I only wish she had written this wonderful book sooner!

~ **Michael Katz**
*Chief Penguin
Blue Penguin Development, Inc.*

FAMILY TYPES

A Guide to Better Parenting Using Personality Types

Selah Rose Cambias
New Orleans • New York • London • Sydney

Copyright © 2013 Selah Cambias. All rights reserved. No portion of this book may be reproduced mechanically, electronically, or by any other means, including photocopying, without written permission of the publisher. It is illegal to copy this book, post it to a website, or distribute it by any other means without permission from the publisher.

Selah Rose Cambias
6601 Veterans Blvd., Suite 4
Metairie, LA 70003
(504) 382-6039
selah@FamilyTypes.com
www.FamilyTypes.com

Limits of Liability and Disclaimer of Warranty
The author and publisher shall not be liable for your misuse of this material. This book is strictly for informational and educational purposes.

Warning – Disclaimer
The purpose of this book is to educate and entertain. The author and/or publisher do not guarantee that anyone following these techniques, suggestions, tips, ideas, or strategies will become successful. The author and/or publisher shall have neither liability nor responsibility to anyone with respect to any loss or damage caused, or alleged to be caused, directly or indirectly by the information contained in this book.

For
Santiago, Maximo, and Isabel.
Without your inspiration, this book
would not have been possible.

Contents

Author's Note	xi
Introduction	1
How to Use This Book	7
Sample Page 1	14
Sample Page 2	15
Part 1 The Family Types Catalogue	17
Chapter 1 The Royalty Types	19
King	24
Queen	30
Prince	35
Princess	39
Knight	43
Damsel	47
Chapter 2 The Feminine/Masculine Types	51
Mother	54
Diva/Goddess	58
Virgin	63
Lover	67
Father	71
Warrior	74
Fool/Clown	80

Family Types

Chapter 3 The Divine Types — 85
- Nun/Monk — 89
- Martyr — 96
- Samaritan — 101
- Priest — 104
- Angel — 108

Chapter 4 The Wisdom Types — 113
- Teacher — 117
- Student — 121
- Seeker — 125
- Hermit — 128
- Storyteller — 132
- Judge — 134

Chapter 5 The Healing Types — 137
- Healer — 141
- Rescuer — 144
- Companion/BFF — 147
- Guide/Mentor — 150

Chapter 6 The Creative Types — 155
- Artist — 158
- Scribe/Historian — 163
- Pioneer — 166
- Networker/Gossip — 169
- Engineer — 172
- Athlete/Winner — 175
- Dilettante — 178

Chapter 7 The Action Types — 181
- Hero/Heroine — 184
- Bully/Coward — 187
- Gambler/Risk-Taker — 191

Rebel/Revolutionary	194
Detective/Spy	197
Midas/Miser	200
Chapter 8 The Wild Card Types	203
Addict	206
Trickster	211
Hedonist	213
Vampire	216
Don Juan/Femme Fatal	220
Part 2 Types for Survival and Self-Esteem	223
Chapter 9 The Universal Types	225
Saboteur	230
Victim/Victor	238
Sell-Out	244
Chapter 10 The Child Types	249
Nature Child	252
Invisible/Perfect Child	256
Magical Child	260
Divine Child	263
Eternal Child	266
Wounded Child	269
Orphan Child	273
Adult Child	276
Acknowledgments	**279**
About the Author	**281**

Author's Note: In order to avoid awkward "he/she," "him/her" references, in some cases we have opted to use either masculine or feminine pronouns for certain examples, usually alternating between the two. The same information pertains universally to both boys and girls. Additionally, where we have chosen to use the word "children," this also applies to parents with one child.

Introduction

"It is a wise father that knows his own child."
~ William Shakespeare, *The Merchant of Venice*, II, ii, 83

Did you ever wish your child came with an owner's manual?

No one knows a child better than his parents. From the first moment we take our baby into our arms, we look for what our child needs and try our best to fulfill it. When our babies respond positively to what we do for them, we feel a great sense of satisfaction. If the baby is hungry and starts to fuss, we pick him up and begin to feed him, and all is well.

But if the baby is hungry and we change his diaper, obviously we will have a less-than-satisfactory result. No amount of cleaning the baby will fill its need for food. And if we can't figure out what he needs, his cries will only worsen.

As our babies grow into children, the same holds true. If we don't know what they're truly in need of, we'll experience more and more frustration.

I distinctly remember feeling frustrated that I was doing the wrong thing again and again to satisfy the needs of my firstborn, Santiago. "I wish he had an owner's manual. I'd know just what to do." I probably said it a hundred times that first year.

Family Types

Then my second son, Maximo, was born 18 months later. This child made parenting look easy. According to many of the parenting books, he was a "textbook" baby. The differences in these two boys were enormous. I called them "yin-yang," "polar opposites," and "meat and potatoes." Santiago made me a good parent by teaching me patience and endurance, while Maximo made me *look* like a good parent because he was so easy to care for.

The challenges I felt with Santiago sent me to the bookstore and to other parents seeking advice. After reading stacks of books and talking to many parents, I was able to pick the things that worked and disregard things that didn't. I realized I had to "write" the owner's manual for my first son. I needed to do what worked for him. Slowly, I figured out his needs by trial and plenty of error. I noticed his patterns and eventually felt much more competent. I even had the wisdom to disagree with the "experts" about some issues because it suited us better.

By contrast, Maximo was predictable and easy to please. He needed only one of three things: food, a fresh diaper, or sleep. Here were two boys, with the same parents, in the same house, but with very different personalities and very different needs.

When my daughter, Isabel, was born, I started looking for her patterns right away. She was strong, but sweet, quiet, and happy. Experience had taught me to work with her natural preferences as much as possible. For example, if she needed to nap, a trip to the grocery store would wait. By learning her expected patterns and working our days within that template, parenting became much easier. I felt like I'd finally figured out a parenting secret.

About the time Maximo was born, I was studying the work of Caroline Myss, particularly her book *Sacred Contracts*. Myss teaches that there are patterns in people that define who they

Introduction

are. Simply "girl" or "boy" doesn't begin to shape us as much as "Princess" or "Queen" and "King" or "Knight."

The psychology of noticing patterns and placing a name on them is as old as Plato. In more modern times, Carl Jung taught extensively on these patterns and used the word *archetype* frequently. But the work of Caroline Myss has been the most impressive and complete of any I had ever read, and as her student I soaked up her work with abandon.

I used her work from *Sacred Contracts* as a guide to help me learn more about my purpose beyond "wife" and "mother." Among my archetypes I found I have an Artist, a Seeker, a Guide, and a Damsel. With her Archetypal Wheel I discovered a new vigor for art, which had been crucial to my well-being. For the next eight years Myss's work became my guidepost. When I thought I was losing myself in motherhood, I used the archetypes as a tool to help redirect me back to the things I needed to include in my life.

For example, I have a Martyr. I would often martyr, or sacrifice, my need for a little quiet time alone because I believed my family needed me more than I needed a break. I was a great mom, giving it all, until one day, I was all spent. I know plenty of mothers experience this. I was everyone's rock so often I had nothing left for me. I was tired and depressed.

I was proud of my strength and endurance that my Martyr gave me, but what a surprise when I learned from Myss's work that I also martyred for the attention it would give me. I thought that if I could live up to "supermom" status, my family would love me and value me more. But when they didn't sing my praises, I would become grumpy and resentful, even blaming them for my exhaustion. My Martyr was simply going too far. What a tough thing to realize, but powerful, too. I made changes to my routine that included quiet and creative time for me. I began to feel more like myself. I was happier and

Family Types

more joyful. The insight I gained from honoring all of me was a lifesaver.

Now I knew if I could learn to recognize the archetype that was giving me trouble, I could change the pattern. I didn't change the archetype; I changed how I behaved and the archetype became a healthier version. *Sacred Contracts* was my guide and counselor, so I decided to go to the source to learn more.

I made my way to Chicago to study *Sacred Contracts* with Caroline Myss at her school, CMED. Even with nearly 10 previous years of use, each archetype came alive like never before. During the year that I traveled back and forth to Chicago, "speaking archetype" became part of everything I did. It was everywhere—at the movies, on TV, in every relationship, and especially in my family. I was living with a collection of archetypes and as soon as I could pinpoint which one was speaking, it was as if I could see their deeper desires.

I learned that my husband has a Rebel archetype, and I saw that he would fight the system whenever he could. Even if the "system" was putting the kids to bed on time so we could relax. It had frustrated me to no end that he would sabotage the routine every night.

Then I realized he was rebelling against the system because he didn't help create it. It was a good system, but even so, it wasn't his. I asked him to help create a new one that included his goals, which involved more reading and snuggle time with the kids. I was actually surprised by how well it worked. We started by getting the children ready for bed earlier, so he would have the time to read and play with them. Bedtime turned into a routine again.

When I saw people through their archetypes, I saw that I could respond to them more effectively. One of my first experiences with using archetypes with children came with my

Introduction

son who has a King archetype. My husband and I called him "the little king" almost from birth because of his temperament and ability to control our attention. When he started bossing his siblings around, I could see that the King was coming out. I knew that a King has a deep need to lead, so I gave him something to be in charge of. Even though he was barely 5, he took on his job like it was his purpose. It was as if he knew he was meant to do it. Each time I would say that I needed someone to be in charge of something, he would step up. But if I commanded him to do a job, he was always reluctant. As long as he was in charge, he would give it his all. I knew right then and there it would be smart of me to figure out the archetypes of all three of my kids and focus my parenting on bringing out the best in each type.

It has been a fascinating and thrilling ride of discovery. Every time I saw a pattern of behavior that I could affix to a specific archetype, I knew exactly what my little one was trying to express. Sometimes it was positive; sometimes the archetype was a challenge. I noticed that each time an archetype became challenging, it was because it needed something. Sometimes it needed to be heard, sometimes it needed responsibility, and sometimes it just needed a better way to get what it wanted. If I could help them become their best version of that type, the problems dissolved.

Every archetype can be a virtue or a vice. Each can be our calling or, if misused, our downfall. But we can't rid ourselves of them any more than we can change our height or eye color. They'll always be with us.

Discovering which archetypes your child has is a fun process. I've written this book for the purpose of helping you, the parent, uncover what archetypes your children have. Each of us will use most of the archetypes at least sometimes, but there is a collection of 12 that we use most often. This book

Family Types

is like a treasure hunt, created for you to browse through and notice if the descriptions sound like someone in your family.

Knowing which archetypes your child has is a powerful tool in helping you understand what he or she needs to feel the most fulfilled. Every human being wants to be loved for exactly who they are. When you can see the archetypes your children were born with, you can give them validation for the very purpose they were born for.

Based on his types, you can guide your child to embark on the path he is meant to walk. And once he is moving in the direction he is meant to go, he will develop a calming sense of purpose. Although we can't expect our children to master their purpose yet, we are empowering them to recognize the best choices for their path and that will serve them their whole life.

Giving them many experiences to practice becoming what they are meant to be, is the highest job of a parent. Accepting that they are learning how to be themselves, but haven't yet mastered it, is wisdom. Knowing how to guide them is powerful.

This book will make you a better parent. It will change how you see your children forever. Once you know what archetypes your child has, and the beautiful gifts that come with those types, you can't help but be the best advocate and support of him or her. What more could a child want in a parent? What more could we expect to be as parents?

How to Use This Book

You do not need to read this book cover-to-cover.

I wrote this book to help parents figure out the personality types or archetypes of their children, and use that information to make parenting easier. When we know their types, we know what is natural and expected from each child. And once we understand the most basic nature of our children, we can work within that nature to guide them to be the best version of themselves.

So how do you figure out what archetypes (or types) your children have?

Although the goal is to find the 12 core types of your child, remember that even learning a few will make parenting so much easier. While we can see our child in many of the types, strive to narrow down the total number to 12. Four of these 12 are universal; in other words, we all have them.

The next eight come from the first half of this book: Royalty, Feminine/Masculine, Divine, Wisdom, Healing, Creative, Action, and Wild Card. (Thank you, Jim Curtan, for breaking these into categories.)

Look at Sample Page 1 (on page 14) for a good format to use through this process.

Family Types

Begin with the Universal types. We all have three of the same types: the Saboteur, the Victim/Victor, and the Sell-Out. These are listed in the second half of the book. Write down these three for each family member. Every person on the planet has these three. They are listed as universal because everyone has these patterns no matter what.

The next step is to pick one from the eight Child types. Each of us has an inner child, but there are many versions of the inner child, including Nature Child, Invisible or Perfect Child, Magical Child, Divine Child, Eternal Child, Wounded Child, Orphan Child, and Adult Child. Read through each one, and pick only one from this group per person.

If your child is very young (younger than 5 years old), it may be difficult to choose a Child type. In time the kind of child they have will develop and present itself, so it may be best to skip this for now. You may find another type in the first half of the book to replace it, or skip it entirely. Either way, this tool will still work exceptionally.

These four Universal types make up the pillars of our self-esteem. We will all struggle on and off throughout our lives with these four types. But in that struggle we can learn self-discipline, personal strength to stand up for ourselves, and unwavering belief in our values. We must each learn to manage these types in order to build self-esteem and self-worth.

Now that you have four types (Saboteur, Victim/Victor, Sell-Out, and one Child Type), what comes next?

After writing down the four universal archetypes, we each have eight more that make us who we are. As a parent you will go on a "treasure hunt" to find the types that best describe your child. Each type is briefly described in the first paragraph. Begin with reading only the first paragraph of each.

If the type sounds like it could be your child, read through

How to Use This Book

the rest. Each time a type sounds right, write it down. Put a star or check next to the ones that seem especially right. You do not need to read this book cover-to-cover. I've made the first paragraph of each type a summery so you can skip the ones that definitely don't sound right.

After you have noted the types that are possible, look at the ones that have a star or check next to them. If there are more than eight, look to see if any of them are redundant.

For example, a Diva and Princess are so similar that one can be removed. Only choose one. Don't worry; you can't get it wrong. All of it helps you understand your child better. And later, if something else seems like a better fit, you can change it.

You're striving for eight types that are all different from each other. If your child is 5 or younger it's perfectly fine to end up with three or four types that seem just right. In time, the rest of his or her personality will show through and you can add to her list.

So what makes an archetype right for your child?

An *archetype* is a symbol that stands for something we generally agree upon. For example, we use the word *king*, and each of us understands that it means something like "the highest, most important one." When we go into detail we may describe it differently, but we all have a general agreement. It is the same when we use an *archetypal* name for our children. We all have seen a little girl that is treated "like a princess," but how that happens exactly with each person will vary.

When you read about the types, envision them as a stencil or common pattern, not as an exact behavior model. Look at the summary and decide if it sounds like your child. The more similar the examples are to your child, the more likely he or she has that type.

Family Types

What if an archetype sounds like your child, but it's the wrong gender?

Any archetype can be male or female. The genders that I use in this book are only there to simplify the writing. Feel free to exchange any male archetype to female, or vice versa. For example, a Gossip isn't always a girl, and a Warrior isn't always a boy. I've met both boys and girls for each.

What if you don't want your child to have a type?

When our children were born we didn't get to decide what their eye color would be, or whether they would be tall or short. It is the same with their archetypes. They came this way, and there is no changing the stencil, or natural patterns they were born with, *but* we can bring out the best in them by giving them a channel and focus for their less-desirable traits. It is a brave and wise parent who is willing to see and accept a challenging aspect of his or her child, then take helpful actions to bring out the child's best.

What if you really want your child to have a certain type? What if you know they should have it?

Often we see what's missing in our children and we instinctually want them to develop that trait. For example, our little King is demanding and we wish he were more like the sweet-talking Prince. But we can never make a King into a Prince. A King won't do anything to satisfy another if he is commanded or cajoled. We will only find rebellion and resentment from him if we press him to act like someone else. He will, however, learn the art of fair mediation and service as a leader if he is shown that he will be a better leader because of it.

Once we are willing to accept who our children are, we can help them become the person they are meant to be. This is the most important and powerful element of this material. It is the

How to Use This Book

key to transforming a challenging relationship into a fun and peaceful one.

Do you pick one type from each category?

The remaining eight types that each person has will come from the rest of the categories. Although there are eight categories, you will not necessarily choose one from each (although you may).

Although this material is extensive, it is not exhaustive, and you may see even more in an archetype that your child has. Because a whole book could be written about each one, feel free to add more description of how your child expresses each type.

Deciding what types your child has is like a treasure hunt. Don't worry that you may get some of them wrong. You can go back and change it later if you discover a better type that fits. It's a puzzle, and you get to decide what makes the most accurate picture.

Remember to look for who they are, not who you wish they are. Don't worry if you decide on a type that seems negative. Every type has both a wonderful and challenging side. Every type carries a gift that will make your child empowered, successful, and happy if we are willing to look for the good and practice bringing that out.

Now you think you know the 12 archetypes of your child. What do you do with that information? How can it help you?

When I work with clients, we use a binder with one page for each type. So after you've narrowed down the types to 12 for your child, create one page for each type. Use Sample Page 2 (on page 15) as a model for those 12 pages. This section will help you articulate the good, the not-so-good, and the actions you can take in response to the archetype.

Family Types

Begin with describing the good aspects of the type if you can. How is this type a good thing? How does it benefit your child? Sometimes it's easier to describe when the archetype is misbehaving. If that's the case, then begin with the challenges and difficulties of the type, then return to the good aspects of it.

For example, your Warrior is very rough when he plays with others and it's hard to see how that type is beneficial. Write down the ways your child is a Warrior and what you find disturbing about it.

Read the example of the good side of the Warrior. Once the negative aspect is out and on the paper, it's often easier to see the positive side. Suddenly you remember that he will bravely stand up for others and has always been able to do that. Write that down as a positive trait.

Finally, use the information you now have of how your child expresses the Warrior and plan a strategy that will address the negative side when you are faced with it.

You may discover that he just has a lot of energy and strength but he also loves to help people. He may need lots of space with few obstacles in the way. But when you're stuck in a challenging environment, maybe now you can look for a way he can help someone. By understanding that he will have this physical energy and strength all the time, you may discover it's futile and even silly to try to "make" him keep still and be careful.

If a plan of action is laid out while things are going well, you will be in a proactive and empowered position. Children often express challenging behaviors at the worst possible moments, when we don't have the time to stop and figure out what they need and decide how o handle it. But if you use this method of preplanning your actions, the situations that cause stress will be alleviated because you will already know what to do.

In my coaching work I have found that nothing is more

effective than having the wisdom to know what's going on and a plan of action ready to use when the issues come up.

Have fun figuring out who your children are, and take a little time to plan how you can handle the tough times, and you'll be well on your way to finding more joy and satisfaction in raising your children.

For more information on using archetypes to parent, please visit my website (www.FamilyTypes.com). There you will find more information, e-courses, worksheets, workbooks, group classes, and private coaching sessions.

I know from firsthand experience how transformative this work is and how quickly it empowers parents to be all we dreamed we could be to our children. If you are struggling with your child, at any age, learning what their types are will help you navigate the issues without unnecessary frustration. Parenting is hard, but it doesn't have to be grueling drudgery. With the keys to your child's personality, you can speed through issues and transform your relationship to that of cooperation and kindness.

No longer do you have to wonder, "Why does he act that way?" or "What was she thinking?" No longer do parents have to play tug-o-war, pushing and pulling children to do what we want. Using the wisdom of their types, parents can bring out the best in their child. Now every child can be loved and understood for exactly who they are.

Family Types

Sample Page 1

1. **Saboteur**
2. **Victim**
3. **Sell-Out**
4. **Child** _____
5.
6.
7.
8.
9.
10.
11.
12.

Other possible types:
1.
2.
3.
4.
5.
6.
7.
8.
9.
10.
11.
12.

Sample Page 2

Name of Family Member:
Type:

Positive Example:

Negative Example:

Three possible responses when I see the negative pattern:
    1.
    2.
    3.

Part 1

The Family Types Catalogue

Chapter 1
The Royalty Types

King

Queen

Prince

Princess

Knight

Damsel

The Royalty archetypes are very common; most families have at least one. The Royalty archetypes are the Queen, Princess, or Damsel, and King, Prince, or Knight. A child will rarely have two from this category, but it's possible if there is a strong distinction. For the benefit of this work, don't choose more than one of these per person.

Throughout history every culture has had Royalty archetypes at one time or another. The male or female leader will embody the King or Queen. That type usually feels the drive to establish community and gain power from accumulating followers. The Princess or Prince is the successor to those leaders but not because he or she is drawn to taking charge. Princesses and Princes will desire to accumulate wealth and notoriety. They do not desire the kind of power that comes with responsibility. They would much prefer to explore the world and what possibilities it can hold. The Knight is ready to serve, always loyal and steadfast. He needs a leader, either the Prince or King, and he needs a mission. The Damsel brings beauty and romance to the kingdom. She desires to be the object of a mission, the one who is sought after and desired.

Movies are full of examples of the Royalty archetypes. They're probably the most obvious in Disney princess movies. The Disney princess movies of the 1940s and 1950s were strongly linked to the Damsel type. The Princess/Damsel always needed a Prince/Knight to save her from something evil, and that task was his right of passage. After rescuing her, he was then trusted to run his own kingdom.

Near the end of the 20th century the Princess archetype

Family Types

evolved from the damsel in distress to taking a larger role in her own rescue. The Princess decided she wanted more than just true love; she wanted independence. Very few Princess movies now show the Prince saving the Princess by himself. Modern Disney princess movies include the princess rescuing herself and the Prince learning to listen to his heart instead of muscling his way through the danger.

We can even see that the archetype of the Warrior has merged with the Princess, creating a strong, independent female. This isn't just happening in the movies. More often now, our daughters are born with a sense of independence and self-sufficiency. Little girls are tough and strong like never before. Art reflects life.

The Prince archetype in movies today is often portrayed as a buffoon, like he's following an outdated tradition and hasn't evolved. To become empowered he must recognize what his heart is calling him to do, and then follow it in order to be fulfilled. It's especially prevalent in movies written for the younger generation. The male role does more than seek revenge, or seek his own fulfillment. More often now the script includes taking others along with him on his journey, or accepting the responsibility of others and not just for his own quest.

It is said that the sexes are just flipping roles, and that males are becoming feminized and females are becoming masculine. But it's actually the natural evolution of the human spirit. A Princess/Damsel must learn that her life is hers to manage first, and that's not a man's job. A Prince/Knight must learn that when responsibility comes from the calling of his heart, instead of tradition or worldly success, he can bring a new vibrancy and peace to his kingdom.

Our children are evolving. It's our job to recognize it and help them find the meaning in their struggles. Trust that your

Chapter 1: The Royalty Types

child has been born with a mission. Our society is changing, and it's not necessarily for the worse. It's our job as parents to facilitate this evolution and teach our children the skills they need to usher it in.

King

**He's a natural leader.
He's a high achiever and will take on responsibility others will avoid.**

Is this your child?

The child with the King type is meant to lead. He demands lots of attention and will do whatever it takes to get it. He may be short-tempered and can get frustrated easily if he has to wait. He may want to try to do everything by himself even if it's too hard for his age. He loves to feel special and will strive to be the best at his passions. He expects everyone to notice his capabilities.

"I can do it myself!" may be his first sentence and lifetime mantra. Another favorite is "Can you get that for me?" These boys love to be served.

What can bring out the best in this type?

The most important need of a King is to be in charge. If he can be given a leadership role, he will always try his best. A King will take himself seriously and expect others to as well. He can be very diplomatic as long as people cooperate.

If your King is resisting your demands, try to give him as a choice. He will be much more willing to do something if he has some power over the outcome.

A child with the King type will copy his parents more than you expect. Because parents are in the role of leader at home, it's important to speak with respect to him and around him. He is learning how to be a leader from the primary example in his life: his parents. When a King has a good example of leadership, he will emulate everything about it. If he has fair and positive role models in his life as a child, he will learn to do the same. Then, when he grows up, he will be much loved and respected.

How can this type be a challenge?

He often feels entitled to the role of leader, even if he hasn't earned it. He won't like working for the team unless they follow him. He may easily give up if he doesn't see a way to feel special. To a child with the King type, leadership and achievement are "all or nothing." In other words, he wants complete control or he won't participate. He'd rather not play with others at all if he can't feel better than them in some way.

He may feel very hurt, even worthless, if he thinks people don't see him as better or more important than others. You may be surprised at how disappointed he is by not getting an award, especially if he didn't seem to try very hard to get it. The opinion of teachers and coaches is very important to him. He desperately wants the adults in his life to think highly of him. He won't always work very hard to win their praises, especially when he's young, but he'll expect to get it anyway.

Eventually he'll connect hard work with the rewards of accomplishment and accolades. Once that happens, he'll be hard to slow down. High achievement will be his desire.

It can be difficult to parent a child who believes he should be in charge no matter what. You may find yourself saying: "Who do you think you are?" Well, he's thinking he's supposed to be in charge, and it makes perfect sense to him. He knows he's supposed to lead; he just doesn't realize he's not old enough or ready.

Family Types

A boy with the King type can be very sassy. His tone can smack of "I know what's best, and I don't need you to tell me." Get ready for regular conflict if you intend to show him you're really the boss; neither parent nor child will win.

Also, a King will expect people to just do things for him. You may worry he's a "Mama's boy," and often find yourself serving him even when you know he can get it himself. Parents may struggle to keep themselves out of the servant role, and he can give you quite a fuss when you do. Parents shouldn't worry that they created that spoiled nature in him. You didn't. But when parents are always going out of their way to serve him, it's time to make him do it for himself.

Okay, so now what do I do?

When your son, the King, expects you to serve his every need, he can be very persuasive. When a routine of "he asks, you serve" is established, it could take time to change. Start to make a habit of stalling him. If you can stall him long enough to ask yourself two questions, you can shift this dynamic.

The first question is "Can he do this by himself?" and the second is "Do I want to do this for him?"

If he can do it by himself, he should. Any time you let him take the easy road by letting someone else work for him, he'll lose a little self-confidence. Any boy that has too much done for him, even if he likes it, will start to believe he can't do it at all. These boys desire high achievement; they're made for it. But when you do it for him, he may feel he can't accomplish something bigger on his own. If he can do it by himself, he should, and in the long run he'll build self-confidence.

Additionally if he is able to do a task himself, and you do it anyway, he will learn that pushing people will get him his way. That will be the kind of leadership he learns and uses as an adult. He'll learn that people will serve him if he pushes them

Chapter 1: The Royalty Types

into it. This habit may stay with him even into adulthood.

On the other hand, refusing to give in to him builds feelings of self-sufficiency and, most importantly, respect for others. Once he's completed the task himself, he'll develop consideration for others the next time it comes up.

One of the toughest times to be a parent is when your child talks back to you, especially if you were not allowed to sass your parents at all. If your son is a King, you'll never be able to make him less of a King, and it's likely there will be times when he will get sassy. It's not okay to be sassy, but when you know it's an immature and unskilled way of taking charge, you can use that time to teach him how he can speak to you. When he's disrespectful, it's not personal, but it is the right time to remind him to use respectful language. Anyone who is destined to be a leader will be a powerful one if he can maintain a respectful tone in all situations.

The most effective way to teach a King is by example. Returning his unskilled, even rude requests with an example of how it should be done will diminish his harsh tone dramatically. For example, say: "When you ask me politely, it's more effective. Can you ask me politely now?"

If he's been demanding and abrasive for many years, you may not believe this simple reminder could change him. But the King archetype will want to be the best, and given very little time you will see him strive to improve his speaking style. All children want to be proud of who they are, especially a King. Given the example, he'll emulate it very quickly.

There is one other area a King may struggle with. Work ethic can be one extreme or the other. A King feels entitled to success, so he may not work at it, expecting it to be thrust upon him like a crown. Because a child with the King type expects to get credit and accolades without work, it's important to not reinforce this at all.

Family Types

Today many parents believe that to build the self-esteem in children, we should shower them with compliments. But we're finding that children are unable to accept any critique. A King who can't hear a truthful evaluation will never be able to reach his potential. He won't develop the strength to strive for excellence and overcome obstacles.

But if a child with the King type is able to hear that he did not do enough to succeed, he has the chance to try harder. Once he develops persistence, he will inevitably experience accomplishment. Accomplishment teaches children that they can trust themselves to do their best. When a child learns to trust himself to do his best he learns self-respect. Self-respect is true self-esteem. Don't give him a pat on the back unless he truly deserves it.

On the other hand, parents may find that a child with the King type gives up easily after a critique. Parents may worry that he won't try unless he knows he'll be the best. You may find yourself looking for ways to encourage him and compliment him in order to build his self-confidence. Again, don't praise him for mediocrity. Children can smell out a fake so fast they'll stop believing in your opinion.

Encouragement, on the other hand, should be doled out in vast quantities. But take careful account of how you give it. Be completely honest, and resist complimenting him just to make him feel better. Saying that you believe in him is wonderful; saying that he's accomplished it when he hasn't is damaging.

When your King experiences success, you may notice that he'll push himself more. He'll work harder to experience it again. Tell him you're proud, and tell others about it within earshot of him. But follow up with asking him how *he* feels. He needs to learn how to listen to encouragement from within, and it won't be easy unless he's trained to do so. Ask him what it's like or what he wants to remember about his success.

Chapter 1: The Royalty Types

Naturally, a King wants other people to honor him, but he needs to know that true satisfaction comes from within. His opinion about himself must trump all others. When he knows to listen to his own opinion first, he'll be able to do what's right anytime and feel truly satisfied.

How to be with this type:

If you can step back and think of the King as a calling or purpose, you can better serve the development of that calling. When he's driving you up the wall with his demands and attitude, take a moment to imagine what a good leader is like. When you can model what you want him to be, even when he's rude, you'll create a change in him that's most effective.

Returning his sass with harsh words and punishment may temporarily stop his tirade, but be prepared for a worse one the next time. The only lasting solution to a tyrannical and bossy King is being the example of respect. He will do as you do.

Encouragement is essential, but don't inflate his ego. He may want to hear it, but he'll know it isn't real.

Teach him to listen to the encouragement from within. A benevolent King, kind and generous to all, including himself, is a gift to the planet.

Queen

**She's responsible and likes to care for others.
She has leadership and diplomatic abilities.
She values the well-being of her family and friends.**

Is this your child?

She's so bossy! No matter how young she is, a Queen will try to rule the house. She may be needy and demanding as a little girl, but will become helpful and responsible as she matures. You can depend on a child with the Queen type to take care of things while you're away. She'll be your little helper if you need her. But be prepared for her bossy nature to come out, because then she'll tell you how it's done.

She'll demand attention by any means necessary. She may be a "drama queen" and make a big deal out of nothing. She may play "teacher" as a means to be the leader with an audience. Whatever her way to express it, she wants to call the shots and have it done her way.

She has a sense of perfection and excellence that may cause her to be intolerant of others. She can be very hard on herself as well, and struggle to feel good about her accomplishments. There's never enough reward for her hard work, but she has the potential to become a high achiever.

What brings out the best in this type?

A girl with the Queen type is destined to be a leader. She will

Chapter 1: The Royalty Types

thrive in a role that gives her responsibility and accountability. For all her intolerances of others, she'll have a high standard for herself. She wants to do well, so she will give it her all if she can be in charge. She will naturally bring people together for a common goal, help them organize a project, and keep them focused until it is complete.

A Queen cares deeply for her family and will step in easily when a parent isn't available. She'll seem like a good Teacher or Mother when she's doing this well. She'll seem like an aggressive, nosy boss when she's gone too far the other way. Initially, when someone else is in charge, a Queen may not volunteer to lead, and only step up when asked. But then once she's appointed, she can't be un-appointed. She'll take charge every time from that moment on.

How can this type be a challenge?

All Royalty archetypes have entitlement issues. But unlike a Princess, who feels entitled to stuff, a Queen feels entitled to people following her commands. She can be mistaken for being bossy if others don't want to follow. After all, she thinks she knows best, and she'll say as much.

She doesn't like to be told what to do, either. She may roll her eyes at other authority figures and act annoyed that she has to follow orders. It just doesn't feel right to her to follow, especially other women. If a girl with the Queen type is taking orders from a parent or teacher who has a King, and he is respectful, she'll likely respond well. But if another female is telling her what to do, even her own mother, she may bristle.

Often a Queen will be intolerant of little things other people do. The small mistakes may seem like a giant issue to her because she has a high standard in her mind of what is good enough. Historically, the Queen had a lot of responsibility to care for her domain, and because of that she had to maintain a high standard. So even though your daughter isn't an actual Queen in charge of a land, she will still have a sense of perfection that is higher than others'. She's born with a feeling that only her best is good enough. And in kind, she'll demand it from others.

The temperament of the Queen can spike the emotions of her family members or her friends. She may cause drama frequently because things mean so much to her. A simple family night of going out to dinner may be cause for drama if something doesn't go according to the drama Queen's way.

Okay, so now what do I do?

Some of the perfectionism that is part of the Queen type can be unbearable for parents to watch because it's so extreme. But because this is part of her nature, trying to put a stop to it will wear you out as a parent. Look for ways to show her how much she's already accomplished. Frequently remind her that there are times to just enjoy being good enough. Try to show her how much fun things can be, even if they don't end up perfect. Give her a sense that things will usually work out fine. She'll already be the kind to work hard, so don't worry too much that she'll suddenly stop trying. She won't; she can't. She's the Queen, after all.

Give her many chances to learn good leadership skills. First, teach her to do things on her own. She'll build self-confidence in her own abilities and also an understanding that she's not "above" doing any job.

Then begin to include others in the process. Exceptional teamwork and leadership skills must be learned by experience. A girl with the Queen type is the perfect candidate to learn teamwork skills, because she'll use them her whole life. Once a girl learns to rally people together, she will use that skill far more often than you can imagine. Girls with the Queen type

Chapter 1: The Royalty Types

are the leaders of our future, and it is essential to empower them with compassion and wisdom.

It's important to teach a Queen to be respectful. Your Queen, like a King, will often think she's the best. She thinks she's always that way, and because of that she thinks she must be respected even if she hasn't earned it. She'll often demand respect in a most disrespectable fashion.

Parents who can model respectful language will have an easier time with this type. But it can't end there. Teach her to use respectful language to everyone, even if she thinks she is better than others. This will help your Queen be beloved instead of despised. Give her the language skills she needs to inspire others to follow her.

How to be with this type:

Find examples of other women who embody the healthy leader. Read books on leadership and female leaders. Help your daughter visualize and experience the best examples of strong, healthy leadership. When your daughter can envision her mission and how to accomplish it, she'll feel she's in control and can attain her dreams.

In our culture we don't seem to have as many examples of female leaders as male. That's because when a woman is a fair and strong leader, people think they are leading themselves. Female leaders tend to work in a "team" atmosphere and men tend to have people follow them. Because women tend to bring people together to work toward a common goal, her leadership efforts aren't as obvious.

When a man is a fair and strong leader, we know it and appreciate it. But often a strong, healthy female leader will go unnoticed, or worse, she'll be despised. We don't appreciate strong women yet as a society. Sometimes the role of female leaders is unappreciated because when women are effective,

Family Types

people are brought in as a cooperative group instead of led by one person. The female in charge isn't as obvious.

There is nothing wrong with men leading differently than women. But as young girls, Queens often don't get noticed for this very powerful capability to bring people together in cooperation. Girls may feel unappreciated. It's our job as parents to notice this ability and validate it. Do not underestimate how important it is to tell your daughter that you know what she can do as a leader. When girls hear their parents acknowledge their leadership capabilities, they have been reinforced in a powerful way.

Having a daughter with the Queen type is a heavy responsibility for parents. We are shaping the leaders of our future. And although a good female leader will receive less notoriety for her leadership simply because she's female, her ability to include everyone may make her less noticed, but no less powerful.

Assure your daughter that, although she may not get the same recognition that a man would, at least at first, the world is changing and in need of her kind of leadership. She is creating and defining a new way to lead, and the world will be better because of her.

Prince

**He is the "golden boy," self-assured, sweet, and independent.
He's attractive, charming, and always ready for adventure and something new.**

Is this your child?

He likes attention, a lot, but he's not needy. He's independent and will do things his way, even if his parents don't like it. He's adventuresome and loves exploring new places. You can take him almost anywhere because he can get along with most people. The mother of a Prince is his greatest fan. She'll dote and give him whatever he wants just to please him.

Making friends comes easily to a Prince. He'll always have people who follow him. He won't tell them what to do, and he doesn't care much what they do, as long as they don't boss him around. He's not thoughtful of others, but he does love people. More often, though, people love him.

What brings out the best in this type?

A Prince must explore "new lands" and even occasionally "slay the dragon." He needs wide area to play in and new things to try. A Prince will not feel like staying home; he'd rather get out and go. His home may be a fun place to be, but he'd rather visit somewhere else. A favorite word for a Prince is "freedom." He's most himself when he's out in the world.

Family Types

Because he's so charming, a Prince will make friends easily. He'll adapt to new environments, and people will accept him into their groups willingly. He may be given a leadership role, but he won't ask for it. He isn't interested in perfectionism from other people, and he doesn't need things to be done "just right." He does, however, want to be seen as perfect. He loves to be admired. As his parent, you'll often have people tell you how wonderful your son is.

How can this type be challenging?

His passion for all things new and undiscovered is the most important thing to him, even if it's inconvenient to other family members. He may bug his parents incessantly to go somewhere fun and interesting no matter the cost. He may have no clue that he's expecting too much of others and seem very insensitive.

A Prince feels entitled to anything he wants. If he sees it and wants it, he'll tend to just take it, thinking it's no big deal. It's in his nature to expect things to go his way even if you never once indulge it. He won't demand like a King. He doesn't command people or ask others to do things that serve him. He will just take what he wants instead. Then he'll be surprised that someone is upset about it.

For example, he may expect to get a turn with a toy, and take it when he thinks it's time. He won't worry what other children want, and if they are upset it won't make sense to him. He won't be too upset either, if others are careless with his things. After all, he'll just get another.

As a Prince grows up, he'll be less available to his parents, and it may feel like he doesn't care. He won't volunteer to help or ask about how his family is doing. You may find that the only time he spends with his family is when he can get something out of it. It's very common for the mother of a maturing Prince to feel like the sweet little boy, who was so fun and easy to take places, has moved on and forgotten her.

Okay, so now what do I do?

Once a Prince reaches his late teens, he will inevitably go through a phase of complete self-indulgence. It's necessary for him to satisfy the feeling that he has made his own life on his own terms. Trying to work within his desire for independence will save a lot of heartache. Once he's an adult, the less you stand in the way of his choices, the less he'll push you to let him make them.

Most parents don't want to hear this, but a Prince won't likely follow too many rules. The fewer rules you have, the more fun you have parenting a Prince. It's not that he's being rebellious; it's just that he's out for fun and adventure. It will be easier for him to fit in with the family structure if the family wants to have a good time, and actively seeks enjoyment. He'll want to please people, including his parents, if he knows it will bring him fun and freedom in return.

Because a Prince is always on the go, he won't want to keep his things in careful order. If it becomes a battle to get him to clean up, help him remove any extra things from his room. A Prince doesn't need as much stuff as most people. He travels light because he expects to get what he needs from others. Keeping his belongings to a minimum will give him more freedom and be less of a struggle for you.

Some parents use the consequence of taking away freedom from a Prince in order to get him to do what they want. Tread very carefully here. It is never good to set up consequences that oppose the nature of your child. Although it is necessary to hold him to rules, it's easier to get the results parents want if following the rules will lead to the reward he holds dear. Avoid making your home his prison.

Family Types

How to be with this type:

Parents will never worry about whether the child with the Prince type will land on his feet or not. His ability to go out into the world and take it on will be the strength that carries him for the rest of his life—that is, unless we make the mistakes of undermining his independence and crippling him with too much doting. It's so easy to spoil a Prince by giving in to his every desire. He's so charming and sweet even the toughest parents can't always resist. But if he's given too much, without having to work for it, he'll become lazy. As with any overindulgence with children, the worst part is that they'll stop believing they can do things for themselves at all.

At home he needs a fair share of responsibility, but not as a leader of others. Give him his own jobs, or chores, and allow him to accomplish them his own way. This will reinforce that you trust his ability to make his own choices, yet still hold him to the family dynamic. He needs independence and freedom, but he also needs to learn that independence and freedom can coexist with living and cooperating with others.

Find ways to embrace his independence and make allowances for his free spirit. He'll feel most comfortable with people who aren't trying to change him. It may sound strange, but the Prince will teach his family to love unconditionally and expect nothing in return. It is a much harder lesson than most people imagine, but once it is accomplished, every family member can learn that true love holds no one back from being exactly who they are.

Princess

**She has self-confidence, tenacity, and a bold sense of belonging.
She has a taste for the good things in life.
She knows what she likes and dislikes.
She will refuse to step aside and let another put her below them.**

Is this your child?

The little girl with Princess type will have to be the center of attention in most circumstances. She may be Daddy's Little Girl. She'll push away her siblings to be his one and only, or do all the things he finds fun. She'll love receiving gifts and will even ask for them. She loves dressing up, but it has to be her choice. The girl with the Princess type gets noticed.

The parents of a Princess may have never spoiled her with gifts, but she'll never pass up a chance to buy something new. She'll measure her worth by the material objects and clothes she has in her closet. Her looks are very important and very personal. She can be insistent about what she wants to wear and try to bend the rules about what's appropriate.

What brings out the best in this type?

As much as your Princess wants something new, she also loves to give others new things. She'll seek approval by giving away her things, and even giving away her parents' things. She

Family Types

may learn to create things that she can give away instead of giving away what was bought for her.

Grandparents typically enjoy buying things for her because her response is usually delightful. And when she wants to share feelings of affection, she'll take the time to make them a card or craft.

She loves to be the favorite, especially of her dad. She needs to know she is special in some way and will work very hard for this status. She will adapt an interest to a sport or hobby that her father enjoys. It's nice for a father to share his favorite activities with his daughter.

How can this type be a challenge?

A Princess will be tender to those who need attention, whether friends or family, as long as it doesn't cost her too much. She thinks highly of herself, and it's an effort to extend compassion to a sibling that competes with her for her parents' attention. She'll have many friends, but she'll be intolerant or snobby of people who seem "below" her. Children who whine or tattle are particularly annoying to a Princess, even if she does it, too.

A Princess is never completely satisfied materially. When she asks for a gift and receives it, she may seem happy for a little while. But inevitably she'll ask for something else much too soon.

She'll also expect others to take care of her things. She may not be messy, but she will expect others to want to help her clean up. She can be oblivious to a hardworking parent. Mom may ask her to clean up while dinner is cooking. The Princess may expect Mom to stop and help her. Most children don't have the ability to recognize how much a parent is doing, but a Princess will be exceptionally out of touch with the labors of others. She may even tell others to do things for her without the least hint of concern for them.

Chapter 1: The Royalty Types

Okay, so now what do I do?

She may never be a naturally considerate person, but she can be taught to think of others, and in doing so she will find a deeper satisfaction in her relationships. Parents need to be respectful when they ask her to do her part. This role modeling is very important for a Princess. She needs to hear many examples of how to ask people to do things with kindness and respect. Because she will always have a tendency to ask others to do things for her before doing them herself, these language skills are vital to her success and happiness. Without them she will spend a life wondering why so many people are uncooperative and mean to her.

Princesses don't tend to want to do what they're told, especially by their mom. Before you get too frustrated, recognize that she comes this way, and she will never willingly do what she's told. On the flip side, she will flourish in situations that give her independence and choice. Find a way to ask her to do a task that involves choosing. For example, say: "You need to pick up your room and do your homework. Which one would you like to do first?" Any time you make the effort to feed her desire for independence she will feel trusted and understood.

Raising a Princess will include some tug-o-war no matter what. It's important to pick the times when it's worth it and to seek as many chances as possible to have her feel in charge of herself. Few but firm boundaries are easiest to enforce for parents—and easiest to follow for a Princess. Parents need to communicate that they are purposefully giving her the choice instead of giving in.

Another effective way to do this is to put her off when your Princess starts to push and insist on her way. Use the phrase "I'll think about it and let you know." Whatever you decide,

Family Types

even if you're letting her have her way, it came from you, not from her pushing you.

If there are many good, cooperative experiences between a Princess and her parents, the foundation of trust and respect is built. Then when parents must draw the line, it will be easier. It's much more effective than never allowing a Princess to be in charge "because I'm the mom" and constantly butting heads.

How to be with this type:

When she's asking to go shopping for something new yet again, she may need some one-on-one time. Her craving for material objects is code for needing love and attention. Take some time, even a half hour, to talk to her and ask her about her day.

Teach her to give to others when she wants attention. The act of giving will reward her the same way, if not better than, getting a new item.

Don't think you spoiled her and made her materialistic, but don't feed her craving for material items either. Her thirst for something new can be fulfilled many ways. Take some time to plan options. Even having weekly game night where she chooses the game can fill her need for connection. To feel satisfied, a Princess must have a gift of the self, like a giving of time and attention. A Princess will help remind parents how much they are truly needed and loved. No item will replace the contact and comfort of Mom or Dad.

Give her jobs that make her responsible for the well-being of others. This will help her develop empathy and an open heart. When she cares for others and feels the reward of their appreciation, her need for material things will diminish.

Knight

He is loyal, hardworking, always willing to help, and he has a strong sense of right and wrong.

Is this your child?

The Knight loves to help, especially if he can be part of a team. He always wants to be part of the action and not left on his own. He's a "man's man" and usually has many friends. Once he decides what is right and wrong, he sticks to his values. He loves to follow a leader, and he's fulfilled if he can be the right-hand man.

A boy with the Knight type will be the first to notice if someone is in distress and will want to help. He can be belligerent and stubborn when he thinks he's right. He feels rejected if he is trying to help someone who doesn't want it.

What brings out the best in this type?

A Knight loves, loves, loves to help. He feels valuable when he can fix a problem. Give him a task that would make your life easier, and then tell him how helpful it is. This is the most rewarding experience for him. A Knight needs a "damsel," like when Mom asks him for help. He needs a "dragon to slay," or a task. It can be something as simple as loading the dishwasher for Mom. Feeling needed and useful is vital to the Knight's happiness.

Family Types

Make sure the Knight has people in his life. He needs a regular group to hang out with. Group sports are just his speed. As a little boy, he'll be drawn to men in uniforms like policemen, firemen, the armed forces, EMTs, and doctors. Any collection of people, particularly people who serve or rescue the community, will catch his attention.

How can this type be a challenge?

A Knight can be very stubborn when he thinks he's doing what's right. He'll stand by his values completely unable to see someone else's perspective. He can be condemning if he thinks someone is wrong, even insisting they change their beliefs. He's the type of kid who would speak out and embarrass parents by saying they're not telling the truth. When the parent tells him to be quiet, he gets louder. Often he doesn't know the whole story, but he'll make a judgment anyway and stick to it.

He may jump in to protect others even they don't ask for help. If his help is rejected, his feelings could be very hurt. He may not understand why someone would refuse to let him help. He always thinks he's on the right side and knows when people need assistance. Even with the leader he chooses to follow, he's protective and self-sacrificing. He may be willing to lie if he thinks it's for the right reasons.

The archetype of the Knight is meant to follow a leader. He is happiest with someone who leads him into adventure and play. He may pick a leader that isn't kind to him, but he'll let that happen just to stay friends. If his leader is a bad influence, a Knight may justify those actions and follow him willingly. Loyalty is so strong in him it trumps good judgment.

Okay, so now what do I do?

A Knight needs to practice thinking for himself instead of following someone else blindly. While he is young, a parent

Chapter 1: The Royalty Types

can help a Knight develop his intuition and self-preservation. When he talks about what he and his best friend are up to, use that time to ask him how he felt and if he wanted to do the things they did together. Usually he does, but pointing out that his own choice is important will help him begin to think about what he prefers. Gently remind him that he can make his own choices, even though they may not be the same as his friend.

A Knight will also need to learn that sometimes people don't want his help. He may take a lifetime to learn this, but plant the seeds while he's young. Teach him to wait until someone asks for help instead of assuming he or she does.

Another useful skill he'll need is learning to ask first if someone needs help. Because he's so quick to jump into a situation at the first sign of distress, he may not be welcomed. But when you give him the language to think and ask first, he'll be able to help those that need it the most.

One of the most difficult challenges with a Knight is his stubbornness. Once he thinks he knows what's right, he'll stick to it. You know you've come up against this when you feel like you're battling with him to make your point. The minute you know you're both locked into a clash of wills, get off the battlefield. End the discussion right there, and tell him you'll talk more about it later. You can almost imagine the armor and shield he's wearing when he becomes that stubborn. He's in "battle mode," and there's no backing down.

But there is a secret to a Knight who is in battle mode: He will take off that armor at some point. Waiting until he does helps both of you find a way to exchange ideas without fighting about it. When you both have calmed down, much later, you can ask if he would talk with you about the disagreement. If you start to bring it up, and you're confrontational at all, he'll pull on his protection and become defensive again. So do it gently, and usually he will be willing to listen. This is great practice for him for when he gets older. He needs to know there are times he can "take off the suit of armor" and be vulnerable. If he can experience discussions with his parents where he's safe to be wrong or vulnerable, he'll be able to do that when he's an adult.

How to be with this type:

Loyalty is the Knight's strongest virtue, and showing him you appreciate that is important. He'll be there for you forever. By letting him know you value him, you give him the capacity to feel loved and respected.

The hardest gift, but perhaps the most important, is showing the Knight that he can make mistakes in judgment and come back without shame. If you and your Knight end up in a battle of wills frequently, always look for a way to let him know you honor his sense of right and wrong even if you disagree. After both of you have calmed down, share how you see his perspective and also how you have your perspective.

In the end, though, be honest with him if you've made an unfair judgment. If he knows you are willing to speak about your own mistakes and make amends, he will have the freedom to do the same as an adult. And once he's grown he'll be able to live without the armor and stay off the battlefield in his most important relationships.

Damsel

She's the quintessential female, soft-tempered and gentle. She loves all things that are beautiful.

Is this your child?

Damsels are delicate and passive, sometimes even quiet and shy. When we have a Damsel as a daughter, we often assume she is fragile and needs to be protected, especially when she is young. She may be acquiescent and rarely speak up for what she wants.

A girl with the Damsel type may be clingy and needy as a baby, and as she grows she'll always feel safer if someone is looking out for her. She's generally obedient and will check in with her mom or dad before trying anything new. She won't push to become independent even if she would like to be.

What brings out the best in this type?

As a young child, the Damsel can be sweet and easy-going. She will easily do what she's told; there's no rebellion in this type. As she matures she'll look for a strong, male role model to help her define her worth. If Dad is her choice, and he is happy when she behaves, then she'll try to behave in order to get his approval. As a parent of a Damsel you may have many easy years with your compliant, "good" daughter.

Damsels value beauty in all forms. She will learn manners easily if she's taught that they make her more attractive. She'll appreciate a beautiful environment and allow her parents to dress her up when she's young. She may go a little over the top with makeup once she's old enough to wear it, but she'll listen to advice from others that she trusts to know better.

How can this type be a challenge?

A Damsel instinctively expects to be taken care of. No matter how old or independent she gets, she'll want someone to lean on. Although a healthy relationship involves being able to support each other, if one person becomes over-dependent on another, the strain can be too much. A Damsel can become so wrapped up in feeling helpless, she may lose her self-worth and become too dependent on others.

As little girls, Damsels will attach themselves to stronger-tempered friends. A Damsel may end up bullied because she lacks the will to stand up for herself. It can be challenging for parents to see their daughter pushed around, even if it's just emotionally. These first friendships will make a Damsel seem more fragile and vulnerable.

A Damsel will work very hard on her physical attractiveness. She believes only beauty is valuable and only beauty will save her. It's no wonder girls dress up so much for dances, parties, and social events. They think they can finally be seen for how beautiful, and valuable, they are. We want our daughters to know there is more to her value than beauty. But convincing a Damsel of this can be difficult.

Okay, so now what do I do?

A girl who keeps herself attractive is not negative, unless that's the only thing she values. A girl who is the Damsel type needs to be reminded that she has many gifts and given opportunities to shine. When she can tap into her other talents and abilities, she'll experience concrete evidence that she's

Chapter 1: The Royalty Types

more than a pretty face. What other ways does she shine? Is she a great problem-solver? Maybe she's creative or athletic. Maybe she's also a teacher or nurturer.

Remind her often that she's so much more than a pretty face. When she's in a crisis over a bad hair day, tell her that true beauty is how she makes others feel. Giving someone a genuine smile will make her seem lovelier than having perfect hair or makeup.

Teach her that she can use her beauty inside to make others feel loved, and in turn she will feel loved. For example, even as a young girl, she can learn the art of listening. People think that women who listen to them are beautiful. If you can help her define beauty in a way that's timeless, she will always feel good about herself. Wise parents give her good tools that last her whole life.

The art of being feminine includes self-care. Young girls will listen to us, but they also watch how we treat ourselves. As mothers, we need to be nurturing and gentle with ourselves, even saying out loud that we feel pretty. Taking the time to exercise and eat right isn't just something extra. If the mother of a Damsel doesn't feel good about herself, a Damsel may learn that she can never be satisfied with how she looks. But when a mother expresses contentment with herself, this model is the most powerful example a Damsel can see.

The Damsel will abdicate her power of choice very easily. She often thinks that someone else knows best, or that people won't like her choices. To a Damsel, when someone doesn't like her choice, it also means they won't like her. When she is young, have her choose often. This will help her develop the confidence to speak up for herself. She'll often resist, claiming she doesn't care. Make her choose anyway. She needs the practice.

Family Types

How to be with this type:

Because we have grown up with the fairytale version of a Damsel, we may just expect everything to fall into place. "Beautiful, sweet girl meets handsome and responsible Prince, or strong and gentle Knight, and they live happily ever after." Hopefully our Damsel daughters will find the perfect match, someone who takes good care of them forever. Eventually, though, they will have to make it on their own at some point, and it's our job to give them the tools.

Help her see and use all her talents and abilities, especially those not related to her beauty. She may tend to neglect and forget she has them. But they will help her experience a full and satisfying life.

Give her many definitions of beauty, particularly the ones that last forever. Anyone who can make others feel noticed and appreciated can also bring beauty and love into the world. And that can be done no matter how beauty fades.

A Damsel will always have the desire to be noticed for her appearance. Help her see that she is beautiful by telling her as much. Although she may feel like it's never enough, she will hear and remember the compliments of her parents. It will help her to obsess less about her looks, and turn her attention to other things.

As long as she has parents that are caring and supportive she'll likely ask for advice from Mom and Dad long after she's grown. If parents do give her advice, it's best leave the final say in her hands. She needs to live her own choices as much as possible.

With these keys you can free your Damsel from the "tower," allowing her the freedom to be all she can be. This is the way parents can give the gift of true beauty.

Chapter 2
The Feminine and Masculine Types

Mother

Goddess/Diva

Virgin

Lover

Father

Warrior

Fool/Clown

Although the word "feminine" suggests that the archetype is for girls and "masculine" is for boys, the types in this chapter are universal. Even though I often use a masculine or feminine pronoun, you can replace those with the other if it fits your child.

I've known many Warrior girls, and yet we often think of Warrior in male terms. The Virgin seems to describe a female, but it can be a male (and often is). I believe only the Mother/Father fall most frequently in their gender, but that's because their attributes are similar. Both are nurturing and protective.

When trying to decide what type your child is, it is likely that at least one from this category will be in their chart. Don't be surprised if there are two. A person can even have two opposing types, like the Lover and Warrior. But if the child seems to have both Lover and Goddess, there may be too much overlap, so choose only one of those two if it seems redundant. Sometimes, though, two similar types are so distinctive and come out in very different ways that it would serve to include them both.

No matter which ones you choose to describe your child, using this material will always lead to better understanding and insight. Look past the literal interpretation and see if there are behavior patterns that are consistent with a type. Can you name at least three times your child has used that pattern in recent memory? If so, you may be looking at one of their types.

Mother

**She loves to nurture and care for others.
She's partial to babies and new life.**

Is this your child?

The little girl with the Mother archetype loves babies. She just loves them. She plays "Mommy," either with dolls or pets, and she's good at caring for younger siblings. You'll see her feed, clean, and tend to her toy dolls. Most little girls like to play house for a little while, but the child with the Mother type will keep herself content for hours with a play kitchen or nursery. She's a great help at home, and loves to help her mom care for her brothers and sisters.

What can bring out the best in this type?

The beauty of this archetype lies in her desire to nurture others. She thrives on learning how to tend to the needs of her family and friends, and will feel most satisfied when given the chance to do so. She enjoys helping her parents with younger siblings particularly when it's feeding or bath time. Whenever possible, find a way to include her in those tasks.

If there is no sibling or pet to tend to, the child with the Mother type will love learning the art of cooking and cleaning. If the act of housekeeping is presented as nesting and tending to the family's needs, she'll enjoy it. If it's presented as a chore, she may not enjoy it so much and prefer other tasks that represent nurturing.

A child with the Mother type loves to learn how to cook almost as much as cradling babies. It's such a pleasure for a parent to have this type of child in the kitchen because she's so hardworking. As she matures into a teenager, trust her to create a family meal by herself. It builds her self-worth. A child with the Mother type is most fulfilled when she knows she is competent at caring for others.

How can this type be a challenge?

The child with the Mother type may become so comfortable nurturing others that she neglects her own needs. To her, being useful is the same as being loved. She may develop such a strong desire to be useful that nothing else satisfies her. Growing up feeling loved *only* when she's useful may stunt her ability to feel love in other ways. She needs to spend a balanced amount of time developing other passions and talents. The ability to care for others doesn't always translate into self-care.

Another negative tendency for the Mother type is using food as a means to feel nurtured. She will love to cook if allowed in the kitchen, but she'll also love to eat. She'll be especially drawn to the foods used as a reward. Sweets like cookies and cake, or salty processed foods like chips and macaroni and cheese give a rush of endorphins, a feel-good hormone. The connection between sweet, starchy food and good feelings is very powerful. It is not that parents caused this. The Mother type has such a strong propensity to connect food with love that it's inevitable. But it is a parent's job to recognize the tendency and help the child learn the difference.

Family Types

Okay, so now what do I do?

Give your daughter the chance to care for others. Building her mothering skills with real life experience builds her self-confidence. She's destined to be a giving person, so teach her how to care for others with competency. She'll watch what her mother does and emulate it. Once she starts helping, let her practice and learn. Including her in the care of the family fosters a peaceful connection between parent and child.

All of us have a range of gifts that we're born with. Sometimes, though, we stop looking for them when we've experienced so much joy from one. Because motherhood is such a common experience, we may think that being good at it is all that's necessary for a girl to be happy. But if the child with the Mother type only feels competent as a mother, she will become too dependent on it as a means of self-confidence. Discover the other gifts and talents she has. Who else is she other than a Mother type? Help her develop those so she can be proud of herself for more than one talent. The more interests she can explore during adolescence, the more the world opens up with opportunities to find happiness.

The kitchen is the heart of the home, and anyone who loves to create nourishment and share it with others is a gift to everyone. Additionally, giving children the skills to feed themselves is vital to developing independence and maturity. With the Mother type, it's important to teach her to focus on food as a means to good health. If she learns to nurture people with healthy food, she can feel satisfied by knowing she's taking good care of them. Help her connect good health and nutrition with good mothering. If she only helps make cookies and connects joy with creating treats, she'll have a harder time as an adult feeling good about serving and eating healthy food,

Chapter 2: The Feminine and Masculine Types

so teach her to cook, and put emphasis on healthy food and healthy nourishment.

How to be with this type:

If your child has the Mother type, you are very blessed. She'll be a help and a joy to the family. Take the time to teach her the skills of nurturing others and she'll feel valued. Remind her to take good care of herself, because it builds her self-esteem. Look for more personality types in her other than the Mother.

Developing other capabilities gives her a chance to find joy in many forms, and not just one. Teach her that good mothering is synonymous with making healthy choices. Her ability to feed herself and others life-giving food is part of her calling.

Diva/Goddess

**She can be athletic and feminine at the same time.
She's naturally self-confident.
She loves to be in the spotlight.**

Is this your child?

The girl who has a Diva type is born knowing she has something special, and she must show it to the world. These girls are drawn to the limelight and bask in it. The child with the Diva type will ask you to watch her do a fashion show or listen to her sing. She'll want to be in the spotlight almost all the time. She'll talk about being on TV, and jump at the chance to show her stuff. When she gets noticed for a performance, she'll love it, and her energy level will get very high. It's not unusual for most kids to have a dream of becoming a movie star at some point. But a child with a Diva type will have wanted fame and all the attention that comes with it her whole life.

What can bring out the best in this type?

Parents will never have to worry that their daughter will fear public speaking. Where most of us fear to tread, she'll blaze a trail. Because she's fearless and desires attention, any situation that puts her in the spotlight will be heaven. Giving her applause for any little performance will make her heart sing. She's happiest when she knows she's captured your attention, and she needs a lot of it.

Chapter 2: The Feminine and Masculine Types

How can this type be a challenge?

Raising a daughter who constantly needs attention can be worrisome for parents. Left to her own devices, she may experience some of the pitfalls of looking for attention in the wrong places, but channeling her deep desire into some sort of structured performance or expression will yield excellent reviews.

What is healthy attention? How can parents help her get attention for hard work or a quality performance? The child with the Diva type has the energy and desire, but she needs a venue and a plan. That venue can be the living room, with the family's complete attention, for 15 minutes every Friday night. The plan may be dance lessons and annual performances. This type needs to connect excellence with applause. Help her reach for the stars with practice, practice, practice.

Children with a strong desire for attention may have little sense of what is age-appropriate. Although playing dress up and putting on Mom's makeup is fun for most girls, a Diva will want to wear it all the time—even at 3 and 4 years old. She may push hard to be allowed to wear makeup, have long, painted fingernails, and wear sexy clothes. This can be very unnerving and exhausting for parents who want their daughter to grow up slower.

It can also be stressful if your daughter is always looking for attention and any kind is fine with her. Parents may feel like they must always shadow their Diva, lest she find herself in a compromising situation. Often parents feel like they did something wrong. They believe they did not giving her enough attention, and now she's looking for it elsewhere, or they gave her too much attention and now she expects it all the time.

When fear, guilt, and worry take over parenting, we're helpless to see the whole picture, and solutions are hard to see.

Family Types

Children are born with passions and desires, and parenting one way or another didn't cause them. We can't make them a different type, but we can direct their type into a healthy direction.

It's not easy to talk about the feminine allure, especially if a very young girl already has one. We all want our daughters to be sweet, pretty, and innocent, but that isn't always the reality. The power of the femininity is potent, and a girl who carries a great sense of that power must learn to handle it responsibly. This won't happen overnight, and it won't feel like an easy, short-term job for parents to teach, but every effort is worth it.

Okay, so now what do I do?

Believe that your daughter has been given a gift that could open doors for her as she grows up. Many people are afraid of public speaking or performance, but she will never be. She'll always shine. Teach her to present herself with reverence and self-respect.

She'll always go for the easy way to get attention, like sexy clothes or makeup, but what she needs is way to express herself that makes her feel special, and a high-quality performance is the best bet.

Her clothes can be an excellent place for self-expression, as long as she feels special and attractive but not trashy. Parents can be creative here. Exploring the world of fashion and beauty with your daughter can be fun and fulfilling. Check out stores ahead of time that carry appropriate items. Then bring her to them to give her the chance to make a few choices. Whatever you do, do not give in and allow her to pick items you don't approve of. A child who is the Diva type is quite persuasive. Don't give in. Insist she look for fabulous without being frivolous. Add sparkle and shine instead of skin and slink.

A Diva needs a place to shine—a stage to show her stuff.

Chapter 2: The Feminine and Masculine Types

First help her choose a quality way to express herself. Dancing, singing, and cheerleading are all ways to help her feel seen. Hold her to good-quality work. Teach her that channeling her passion for the spotlight into self-discipline will give her a strong foundation to grow on. Anyone can stand looking sexy in the right clothes and makeup, but true hard work and excellence will help her stand head and shoulders above others. And that's right where she wants to be.

How to be with this type:

Parents may feel like they have to be tough and hard-nosed. But after you set very strong boundaries, look for ways she can feel fabulous. Ask her what she likes. Then keep asking her what she likes. Eventually you'll find a place where you both can be happy. Remind her that there are many ways to be extraordinary without having to resort to sexy.

Young girls who turn toward sexiness for attention need to see all the other ways to get positive attention. Take time to think about how your daughter can gain the attention she desires, whether it's in academics, the arts, leadership, or even sports. Ask her if she's interested in any of them, and find a way to get her involved.

At the appropriate time, be brave enough to teach your daughter about how her feminine expression is seen to others, particularly boys and men. Be brave and start early talking about the difference in males and females. A Diva already can sense those differences, and she needs the language to understand it. She feels the power of feminine energy and how it can command attention. She needs to know how to handle it appropriately. If there are frequent, calm conversations about healthy relationships and how to get attention from others, it will be easier to reroute a girl who is beginning to flaunt too much. Don't overreact, but definitely act.

Family Types

A proactive and positive approach will create a wonderful environment for a child with the Diva type to grow up in. It takes a wise and smart parent to handle a passionate daughter with this type. Although it may not feel easy, your daughter will grow to honor the parents who honored her true spirit.

Virgin

**She needs to keep something purely for herself.
He can be stingy with affection.
She may keep certain special items in a secret place.**

Is this your child?

Either a boy or a girl, the Virgin type is not literal, but rather symbolic of the kind of child who keeps something only for himself. A boy may seem shy around others. He'll always regard new people from a distance, and not jump in to be friendly.

A girl with this type may be aloof, and even stubborn about keeping a distance. As a toddler she won't smile at you just because you smile at her. She won't give a kiss even to grandparents unless they scoop in and take it. A girl may refuse to share something because she doesn't want others to touch it.

Boys will be harder to identify as a Virgin type because at a young age we allow them to dislike affection much more than girls. A boy who doesn't like to be hugged or kissed and won't return affection may have this type. He may have a special toy or collection that he doesn't like to show or share. He may seem stingy and protective of a cherished item. If a boy has this type it will be more apparent as he matures.

What can bring out the best in this type?

The child with the Virgin type has a sweetness and

Family Types

vulnerability that is touching. Family members of the Virgin type may be protective of him and the things that are precious to him. If the child with the Virgin type feels safe with someone, he'll trust him or her. For family and friends, it is very satisfying to be trusted by this type.

We often expect our children to learn how to share, but this will seem impossible sometimes if your child has the Virgin type. If family members can allow him to keep some things only for himself, it will help him trust you and then he'll be able to share other things easier. Trust is not easy for the Virgin type; he needs his family to understand and protect him.

How can this type be a challenge?

Even if parents protect a young child who has a special toy and doesn't want to share, we expect our kids to grow out of it at some point. Eventually we may insist they share or we may say: "Just show your favorite doll to Aunt Margie; she'll be careful with it." Even if Aunt Margie is careful, to the child with the Virgin type, the doll will become tainted. The child may become overly upset, and you may have to deal with a huge fit. This can be embarrassing to a parent, because it looks like the child is spoiled. Parents may see the child share other things, but not certain things, and push the Virgin type to share everything. This can yield a strained relationship between parent and child that gets worse as he matures.

Whether a boy or girl, a Virgin will need a piece of himself protected and kept from others. It may be his artwork, or books, or maybe music or writing, but it will be something only he sees and experiences—no one else. Additionally, it doesn't make sense to the Virgin type to open himself up completely and share his feelings or thoughts. He may be aloof and resistant to a parent who wants him to show affection. He may always seem just out of reach and even thoughtless. Pressing a boy who is a

Chapter 2: The Feminine and Masculine Types

Virgin type to be more affectionate may make him feel shame and guilt.

As he matures, a boy with this type may avoid close relationships, and keep only superficial or platonic friendships. Instead of talking about one girl who interests him, he may talk about many. Both boys and girls that have the Virgin type may take longer to start dating than their friends. When most teenagers are bearing their soul to friends with teenage drama, the Virgin will be much more private about his or her emotions. It can be challenging as a parent to decipher what this teenager is feeling and experiencing.

Okay, so now what do I do?

If you're concerned your child may be spoiled and stingy with his toys, take a second look to see if perhaps there are only one or two special toys or items that he wants just for himself. If he isn't stingy all the time, and only with a couple of things, he may just need to be allowed to keep those things for himself. Taking some time to talk with him about the few precious items he can keep private may be enough to remedy the child who is stingy with everything. Try making sure those one or two special items are protected for siblings and others, then gauge how he handles sharing other items.

It may take some time to change his stinginess if all his items have been passed around regularly. Once he knows those special items are only for him, he should eventually find it easier to share. When your child knows he can depend on you to protect his need, he will feel much more willing to open up other areas of his life. He will be more free and generous knowing that something is kept special, just for him.

If the child doesn't like to share affection even with a beloved grandparent, it's better not to insist that he must. Children who are given the choice will eventually feel comfortable on their

Family Types

own to share affection. Though it is never okay for a child to be disrespectful, teaching even a toddler to say "no, thank you" to a solicitation for a kiss is appropriate. The child with the Virgin type is not cold and unfeeling. He or she simply needs to know that he has the choice of when and with whom to share feelings. Allowing him more time to get close to people, even relatives, will help him feel safer and more willing to open up as adults.

The teenage years may be quieter for the Virgin type compared with other kids his age. Although this may seem refreshing, a parent may worry about the lack of interest in dating. The most powerful gift you can give him is a combination of first honoring his privacy, especially about his feelings, and second making sure he knows you love him and are available anytime, about anything. These kids are thoughtful and careful, but still vulnerable to mistakes. Give him lots and lots of info about dating and relationships, but don't expect him to tell you what he thinks about it. Don't push him to go out and have fun; he'll go when he's ready.

How to be with this type:

The littlest ones with the Virgin type need you to help them honor something precious. Whether it's a toy, blanket, or even the choice to give kisses and hugs, if they know they are protected they will feel safe and secure. Once they feel safe and secure, they will find it much easier to share both affection and toys.

Expect them to keep something completely private from you their whole lives. It's not a reflection of your parenting. You didn't make him that way. Honoring that need in them will help you develop a strong, trusting relationship. The child with the Virgin type does not long to be completely open and vulnerable with someone, but does long to know he can be if he so chooses. His first example of that is you, his parent.

Lover

**She has the ability to completely love something or someone without holding back.
She's able to see through something negative for the sake of love.**

Is this your child?

Think *Romeo and Juliette*, love at first sight, and love so deep they were willing to die for each other. When a child has the Lover type, and she falls in love with something or someone, she'll use expressions that convey intense feelings. She could love a pet, a rock star, or the cute boy at school. She'll say things like "Oh, he just so cute, I can't stand it." or "He's so awesome, I'd do anything." She'll speak from the heart with tremendous passion. Like tween girls screaming like crazy for a superstar, it's exactly what a Lover feels like. Her feelings will be *huge*.

A Lover can be a boy or a girl, although you will notice it more often in girls. If a boy is described as sensitive, he may have this archetype. He'll care deeply about someone or something, and as his parent you may frequently want to protect him from having his feelings hurt.

What can bring out the best in this type?

Any child who has the Lover is going to be able to easily get close to people. When you speak lovingly about people, they

Family Types

will feel loving about them as well. If you tell them someone cares deeply for them, they will be able to accept that easily as well. The Lover wants to share love with people, and if your child knows she has a community of people to love and who love her, she will be most happy.

A child with the Lover type needs someone special to love as well. She feels destined to be part of a couple and will look for an object of affection even from a young age. By giving her a special pet or toy, the Lover will be content—that is, until you go on vacation and forget the special toy, or the treasured pet passes away.

How can this type be a challenge?

If the object of affection is lost or passes away, the child with the Lover type will be devastated. Your job as the parent is to help her carry her grief, and that's an especially tall order if you, too, feel heartbroken. The purpose of loving deeply is to live the greatest gift of the human condition. Love one another. The challenging side of this purpose is carrying the heartbreak that will inevitably be part of life. If your child has the Lover type, and you know the she will eventually have her heart broken, the most important role you take is to teach her that people are supposed to comfort people. Taking the time to teach your child how to handle times of grief by reaching out to others for comfort is the most essential tool for the Lover.

Parents may try to avoid the inevitable heartbreak, and refuse to buy a pet or not allow the child to become attached to special items, but eventually they will have to face it. It does no good to keep her from falling in love.

As she matures, girl with the Lover type may become "boy crazy." She can get so wrapped up in fantasies about a boy at school or a rock star on TV that it may seem she can't focus on anything else. When parents try to block the connection, they

Chapter 2: The Feminine and Masculine Types

may experience a rift that leaves the girl feeling more isolated and the parents less influential. Many families experience years of stress and tension during the tween years when parents don't allow a child to fully express her feelings because they are so extreme. While we want our children to learn self-control, keeping them from expressing themselves, especially with this type, can be disastrous.

Okay, so now what do I do?

If you think your child has a need to attach to something with so much passion that she thinks her life depends on it, give her something to attach to. Then give her more. When a child with the Lover type has only one object of affection, she is vulnerable to losing herself in that one thing. When the object of her affection is removed, she will be completely devastated. A child with the Lover type needs to learn that her life must contain many people and passions in order to be most stable. If you worry that getting a dog will break her heart, consider getting two or three. Even if she attaches to one, she'll be able to move on to another easier if they're in her life already.

If you're already struggling with a tween or teen who is crazy for one boy and you want to temper her passion, take the time to find other things she loves to do, and do them often. A child who is the Lover type will have many passions but will get lost in only one if left to her own devices. As a parent, you know your child best; if you can bring other passions to life, it will help dilute her interest in one person or thing, and even give her a strong foundation of support if her heart gets broken.

How to be with this type:

A child with the Lover type is wonderful to have in the family if she's shown that families are made to love each other.

Family Types

Give her affection and confirmation of love by telling her often how much you love her. You can never say it too much. Give her many things to love, and she'll feel most happy and fulfilled. These things can be pets, people, and even activities like art or sports.

If she gets too crazy for someone at a tender age, refresh her experience of her other passions. It will help her keep perspective about all the wonderful things she can love, and love to do. When she experiences a heartbreak, and she certainly will, teach her that it is a time to pull close together and care for each other. She'll remember this as an adult and call you for comfort instead of isolating herself, and that's the most important lesson for a Lover.

Father

He has the ability to nurture others with advice and encouragement.

Is this your child?

The child with the Father type likes to give advice or directions about how to do something. He doesn't like to see people struggle if he can give them some pointers to make it easier. He will notice children younger than he and tend to their needs when he thinks he can help.

He can be nurturing and supportive, even helping when something is being created. He won't necessarily want to take a leadership role. He'd rather watch over and guide. If you have a son who enjoys leading when a group has a goal, you may have a boy who has the Father type. These kids will adore team sports or activities that involve working together as a team.

What can bring out the best in this type?

The boy with the Father type likes to help out other leaders, like coaches, to bring team spirit to a group. He'll thrive doing something that helps others do a task or helps others feel encouraged. He doesn't have to be the boss, but he will become pushy if people aren't working together for the common good. These boys will grow into men who do best in jobs that bring people together to create or accomplish something.

When people need someone to talk to, the boy with the

Family Types

Father type will be a good listener. He won't search out people who need help, but he's always willing to help those who ask.

How can this type be a challenge?

Watch out for times when his authority can go to his head. The boy with the Father type has a very strong belief that he's always right and that he knows better than everyone else. Because he can be inflexible, he may even lose friends who don't feel like following his ideals. It would be useless to tell him he's wrong and that his standards are too strict. If this archetype is within him, he was born to have a strong conviction about his values. Telling him to back down in order to make it easier for the others will only undermine his self-confidence.

If a boy with the Father type decides to organize a team sport he will expect the other boys to follow his rules. He won't consider their opinion as relevant and totally ignore what others want. For the Father, it's not that he wants to be above all others (like a King), but rather he believes he knows better than all others.

The boy with the Father type may have a hard time asking for help when he needs it. He's independent and wise, but sometimes he needs support and will fail to ask. He may struggle with problems alone for too long, believing he's a failure to ask for help.

Okay, so now what do I do?

Don't tell him he doesn't know better than others; you'll end up in a standoff. The Father type's greatest desire is to see the group succeed, and he will be open to learning how to do that if you let him know you believe in him.

Most challenges in parenting come when our children are unskilled at attaining what they desire. All archetypes have a calling or gift that will make the world a better place. The

Chapter 2: The Feminine and Masculine Types

parents' and teachers' job is to help teach our children the skills it takes to act on their calling with wisdom and grace.

A boy with the Father type needs to learn how to listen to others with respect, even if he doesn't agree with them. It will be one of the hardest things for him to do. Teach him that when others know their opinion has been heard, they'll follow a leader easier. After all, there may be other children with a King or Father type in the group, and they think they know what's best, too.

If your son is struggling with a problem and doesn't want to talk about it, he needs to learn that everyone needs support sometimes. If he can see that someone he respects has a confidant, too—someone to talk to—then he may be more willing to talk about his concerns. He won't like to take advice, and it isn't often necessary for this type. What he needs is simply someone to share his troubles with. Being the Father can feel heavy with responsibility. Sharing his feelings is enough to relieve him and help him move forward.

How to be with this type:

Teach him to take a few minutes to listen to the others before he decides what the group will do. This is a powerful tool that brings peace and harmony. Letting others have their say, and even getting the group to vote, is much more powerful and effective than insisting that everyone just does what he says. Help him learn the techniques that bring out the best in a group. The success of the group is his desire, and he's destined to strive for that his whole life.

Make sure he has at least one person, even a parent, whom he can talk to. This person should be a good listener who won't push advice on him, but rather just listens with understanding. The boy with the Father type is wise beyond his years and will usually make the right decisions on his own. Having a network of caring people to support him is all he needs for a lifetime of success.

Warrior

**He has the ability to stand up to someone
for the sake of his values.
She has determination and will to see a goal to the end.**

Is this your child?

Often we think of a Warrior as a boy, but girls, more than ever now, are born with the Warrior spirit. Movies from just 20 years ago would never portray a Princess rescuing herself. Yet today it's more common to see a princess character saving herself than one being rescued. Little girls are sometimes labeled "Warrior Princesses" because they have a toughness of spirit and a mind of their own.

A child with the Warrior type hates when someone is taken advantage of and will be very assertive about setting things right. The Warrior type is often physically sturdy and solid. She may use her physical presence and tough language to say what she thinks. A child with the Warrior type has strength and resilience, both physically and mentally. A girl with the Warrior type may seem stubborn and rough, and never a "crybaby" or fragile. As a boy, he may be like a "bull in a China shop," but also able to bounce back easily after an injury.

What can bring out the best in this type?

The strongest benefit of having a Warrior type in a child is strength of spirit that keeps her focused on a goal. She will

Chapter 2: The Feminine and Masculine Types

have the determination and willpower to stay with something while her friends flounder and give up.

A Warrior will be able to bounce back from injury quicker than most children her age. Little girls with this archetype won't cry about a bump of bruise as quickly as their friends. Both boys and girls will slough off rude comments from other kids easier, too. Children with the Warrior type seem to have a tougher exterior, which can be refreshing, compared with very sensitive children.

How can this type be a challenge?

A Warrior's purpose is to attain a goal at any cost. As a toddler the child with the Warrior type may completely ignore what other children are doing and trample his way into the middle of an activity expecting to join in. He may crash through a game or pounce on top of kids just to be part of the action. A Warrior seems brave and never shy, but also insensitive about what others may be experiencing.

A child with the Warrior type is quick to decide who's right and wrong, frequently claiming that "It's not fair!" If a Warrior has a goal that he believes will benefit someone, he won't stop to think first. He may see someone he thinks is being treated unfairly and jump in to fix it, even if he doesn't have all the facts. He may also have a tendency to strike too hard. He's physically strong and may over-use his strength. He has such a strong sense of right and wrong, his actions will reflect that extreme view.

The child with the Warrior type doesn't notice or care if he's bowled over someone. He may just be having fun, yet he's so rough he tends to hurt his friends. When they become upset he will seem surprised. He doesn't feel pain very easily and will be surprised when others complain of a modest bump that he caused.

Family Types

A Warrior is not born with a sense of empathy, and can seem indifferent and callous to other children. It can be shocking to see his or her lack of response. One of the most important jobs of a parent is to teach the Warrior empathy. Hopefully this can be taught without giving him too much guilt.

Okay, so now what do I do?

The most important need for a very young Warrior is *lots* of room to play. At home, put away the good China and forget about keeping delicate mementos out in view. A Warrior will end up breaking things no matter how many times you tell him to be careful. A child with the Warrior type needs to be sent outside whenever possible to run, climb, and be physical. He needs free time and free space to burn off aggression. Find sports that keep him moving. The football field is a great place to be a Warrior, but beware: In the younger leagues, some kids are not going to be able to take the roughness of a Warrior.

Be prepared to teach the tools of compassion, including how to apologize. If a young Warrior can learn a few techniques that soothe his mistakes, he will be able to give the sport all his passion and still keep his friends.

Many Warriors experience angry responses from parents, teachers, and coaches when they accidentally hurt someone. It seems obvious to adults that a Warrior is careless and even dangerous. Adults will be shocked and annoyed when your Warrior is tearing around, putting other children in peril. With enough of this reaction from adults a Warrior will start to feel limited in places where other children are free. It's common for a Warrior to end up feeling singled out and restricted. Too many instances of this will damage his self-esteem before he has had a chance to develop self-control.

The greatest lessons a Warrior will learn are self-control and empathy. Because he is endowed with actual physical strength,

Chapter 2: The Feminine and Masculine Types

he will have to learn how to handle it before most children his age. No child can learn a life lesson in a day, and it's important to give a Warrior challenging environments incrementally. It's not fair to put a young Warrior in an environment that will require him to use self-control all day, every day.

Developing the feeling of empathy will also take time. Don't expect a Warrior to remember it after one incident. Parents often use guilt and shame to remind a Warrior about how others feel when he hurts them, but those conditions make it harder to sink in. Head off a situation well before it happens. Take the time to talk about how others feel when they get hurt with your Warrior when things are calm. Always make it clear that you know he means no harm, but that he is still going to have to be responsible for his actions.

If your daughter is getting physical in order to have her way, she needs tools to help her get what she wants that don't involve physical action. A young girl with the Warrior type who resorts to hitting or pushing because she wants something she can't have, may not have any idea that there are better ways to get it. What seems obvious to most children may not be so obvious to this type. Frequently reviewing other options, like asking, negotiating, and turning to an adult, will help her hold back physical assertiveness. Her nature is to act physically. It will take time to teach her to use other methods, but she will eventually understand.

How to be with this type:

If you're struggling with the Warrior type in your child, begin with bringing him more frequently to environments in which he can feel free. The mall, an elegant restaurant, or the home of a relative that's not child-friendly will exasperate a Warrior—and likely leave you embarrassed and frustrated. Visiting places like this should be very infrequent and slowly added to regular outings as the Warrior becomes capable. As the parent of a Warrior, it's not fair for you to compare him or her to other children who are able to visit places where he must be completely in control of himself. It's not his fault or yours; it's just his way.

The child with a Warrior will always have very little sensitivity to his surroundings, but as long as he has places to truly feel free, he can learn to use self-control in important environments. Make his home a safe place to relax and be himself. Talk to him about different environments and when he will need to be gentle. I've found that using terms like "gentleman" or "lady" in those environments can help remind them to use self-control. Talk to him before leaving for a challenging environment. Remind him that it's temporary but important for him to be his best and most gentle self. Then reward him with a compliment when he can keep it up longer than previously.

Taking note of when he is trying to be careful and telling him you noticed will reinforce the good behavior. He's probably heard lots of negative comments about his behavior. A Warrior needs to know he's not always messing up. At home when he is tearing up the backyard and feeling free, parents can give him smiles and tell him he looks like he's having fun. Relieve him of feeling guilty every time he is feeling rough and tough.

Teach a Warrior that an apology is vital if he hurts someone or something, even when he didn't mean it. "I didn't mean it" is a common mantra of a Warrior. Of course he didn't, but he still needs to do something to make amends. Standing by, and waiting until the injury is better, instead of running off after an incident is also important. Often a Warrior will say "sorry" and then run off while someone is still in tears. If a Warrior witnesses the result of his mistakes, he can develop more awareness of others. Most importantly, he'll develop empathy instead of guilt. When

Chapter 2: The Feminine and Masculine Types

the injured person can return to play with the Warrior, he can see that his mistakes are not horrible. On the road to growing up and gaining self-control, a Warrior can learn that, although he may be too strong and rough sometimes, he has the inner strength to help fix his own mistakes.

Fool/Clown

**He has the ability to see hypocrisy
and point it out using humor.
He can make people laugh and loves to see people happy.**

Is this your child?

He's the class clown. A Fool is often a boy, but can be a girl, too. He's the one who loves to make people laugh. He'll make fun of anyone's weakness, including his own. He'll sometimes pick on a shy person or mock a conceited one. Most kids won't pick on him because they know he'll poke right back. It may seem like he just wants attention, but there is a deeper purpose to his antics.

Historically, the fool, or court jester, was entertainer to the king. But his more important role was to use humor to tell the king if there was dishonesty in his cabinet. If anyone else simply told the king who was betraying him, it would make the king look like a fool. If the king was shamed, he would throw the person betraying him in the dungeon. Only the jester could expose the betrayer without getting thrown in the dungeon. He would do this using humor, metaphor, and pun.

In the same way, a child with the Fool type uses humor to expose the weaknesses of others. The child with the Fool type has a strong sense of right and wrong. He won't be able to tolerate dishonesty in anyone, especially people in charge of

Chapter 2: The Feminine and Masculine Types

others. That means parents, teachers, and coaches are all under scrutiny by this child.

What can bring out the best in this type?

If your child has the Fool type, your happiness will mean a lot to him. When you are in a bad mood or going through a tough time, his jokes will become more frequent. He's doing that to trying to pull you out of the sadness. So even if his timing and taste are poor, you can appreciate his deep desire to see you happy.

It's helpful to remember that the Fool never wants to hurt anyone; rather, his purpose is to expose weakness. If he's given the attention he needs when someone is falling short of expectations, he'll feel heard and turn his attention to creating laughter. If he knows his parents listen to him and respect his opinion—even if they disagree—he will temper his judgments.

Just as the court jester did so long ago, once the king understood the meaning behind the jokes, the jester could then move on to entertainment. Instead of mean-spirited jokes, the child with the Fool type will use a kinder, gentler humor that can bring people together.

How can this type be a challenge?

At school, the worst side of a Fool will come out if he has a teacher who is weak or disrespectful with his students. A child with the Fool type will notice a weakness in a teacher much faster than other students will. It will almost seem like he's bringing it out and is causing discord. This type can put parents in a very challenging position when he plays the Fool and exposes the teacher.

At home, if the Fool decides to humorously point out weakness in other members of the family, parents may be stuck

Family Types

in the middle again. That could be particularly difficult if he pokes fun of an authority figure like Mom, Dad, aunts, uncles, and even grandparents. He may be pegged as the family "smart-mouth," which is very uncomfortable to deal with.

The worst concern for this archetype is that the child will grow to be disrespectful of all authority figures, including bosses and even the police. When a Fool is left unguided or, worse, if he is unrecognized and punished harshly, he risks becoming a bully, demanding attention in an even more aggressive fashion. He may not develop self-control and the ability to close his mouth when it is appropriate.

Okay, so now what do I do?

When your Fool is creating a disturbance at school or home, take a moment to look for a pattern. Where does it repeat? Is he always poking at the same people or talking about the same situations? Usually he'll complain a few times before taking aim at someone. Who has he been complaining about? The Fool starts making trouble usually after he's been ignored, or when he feels stuck having to deal with hypocrites (at least, he sees them as hypocrites).

Sit him down and give him your full attention. Ask him to tell you all about the situation. It may seem like strange to advise a parent or teacher to give a "smart mouth" kid attention, or even respect, but it has a way of softening his disposition. Use a respectful tone, and really listen to his perspective. Avoid demeaning him or undervaluing his perspective. It will keep him from becoming defensive and sliding into sassy, unrestrained humor. Take his beliefs seriously; he sees the weakness in others clearer than most, although he doesn't yet know what to do about that discovery. Good parenting can help him learn the tools needed to manage his concerns and refrain from offending others.

Family Types

A "class clown" is the modern-day version of the king's fool. In the same way, a child with the Fool type needs his "king" or authority figure to tell what he sees. He needs to be heard, but his words do not necessarily need to be acted upon. And when a Fool knows he's been heard, he feels his duty is complete. He won't need to carry on and on. To the Fool you, the parent, are the authority figure. It's you that he wants to tell, and it's you that needs to hear what he believes. Make it clear that you understand his perspective and you won't judge him for it. You don't have to agree or disagree; just listen and understand.

It's a risk worth taking to give him the full benefit of listening to his perspective. Parents may worry they're promoting his judgmental personality, but his ability to see the hypocrisy in a person was born within him and can never be stopped. It's like someone telling you not to notice the color blue; you can't help but see it. The child with the Fool type can see hypocrisy with lightning speed, and he must say or do something about it. But once it's said and heard, the urge to expose it dissipates.

What if you disagree with his perspective? The Fool does not need to hear he's right all the time. Although he needs to know you understand, you don't have to stop there. This is a great opportunity to teach him that people can disagree and still get along. Explaining that you see things differently should be sandwiched between comments that you understand. A young Fool won't absorb this concept quickly. He may resist anything but his view. Over years of gentle guidance, he can fully integrate this concept. Imagine how much easier his life will be when he can both feel heard and remain open to the understanding that others see things differently.

How to be with this type:

There will always be teachers, coaches, and bosses who are hypocritical and who demand from others what they can't or

Family Types

won't do themselves. What do you hope your child with the Fool type will do when he's faced with that?

The desire to make things right is powerful in our children. Because things are "black and white" when children are young, a Fool may spend a lot of energy focusing his antics on injustice or weakness, but if he's lucky enough to have parents that can listen well, and are strong enough to disagree respectfully, he will have a lifetime of satisfaction.

Fools are smart. Notice how perceptive they can be. Be proud of their desire for righteousness and help guide them away from expressing it disrespectfully.

Finally, have fun with this type! Watch funny movies and shows together. Laugh and share jokes. These kids love to laugh, and it's a lucky parent who enjoys the show.

Chapter 3
The Divine Types

Nun/Monk

Martyr

Samaritan

Priest

Angel

The archetypes that fall under the category of the Divine relate to our children's desire to be of use and service in their life. When children experience a moment when they are helpful to someone, it brings them a feeling of satisfaction. Often, they will talk about how they helped someone, because it feels like an important moment.

Parents could take this moment to notice how their child helped and what kind of satisfaction came from it. This is the chance to begin to understand the purpose they were given to help others.

Take a few moments to think of the ways you've witnessed or heard that your child helped someone. What were the circumstances that your child recognized and knew he or she needed to reach out to another? Was it a situation in which many other people witnessed, but only your child acted as needed? Was your child part of a team or group that helped another? Was it a medical or safety situation? Was it a simple and humble, but meaningful situation? Did your child help with an emotional or encouraging type of situation? How did your child know what to do? Were his instincts working, or was he following directions? Perhaps there was no direction and he just knew what to do. Or perhaps she remembered seeing someone else follow a protocol and knew exactly what to do.

After the situation in which your child helped, how did he or she feel? Was she proud of herself? Did he keep it to himself, and you heard from others? Did she feel sorry for the person she helped and wish she could have done more? Did he talk about it without needing a pat on the back?

Family Types

Most of us will have at least one type that drives us to be of service to others. The most common archetypes of service are in the Divine category. These are not literal "jobs," but rather ways that your child expresses their helpful side. For example, the Priest is not literally a priest, although he may grow up to be one. Having a Priest for a type means that your child has a propensity to listen to the worries of others and give them encouragement. A child with the Priest type may frequently experience other children coming to him with the things that worry them, and he knows what to say.

Another example is the child with the Samaritan type. She will be the kind of child who will reach out to new students to keep them from feeling lonely until they make new friends. She may not even want to be a close friend, and lose interest in the new students once they are established.

Any of these types can be either a boy or girl, and the gender I have chosen is for simplicity in reading, not an indication of male or female.

Although the category of Divine centers around acts of service, many other archetypes can be expressed as a service to others. Types that help others are not limited to the Divine types alone. This category is for those children who frequently help others like it's their job. It's a great place to guide your child in the satisfaction and sometimes pitfalls of serving others.

Nun/Monk

He or she works to model the best qualities of the family's chosen religion or value system.

Is this your child?

When a child has a Nun or Monk archetype, he acts as if he has an important purpose for his life. She may take herself very seriously and believe she has to live a standard of high moral values in order to qualify for the blessings she receives. Nuns/Monks seem older and more mature than their years, and are drawn to virtue like bees to honey. They strive to serve their religious affiliation in some tangible way. They do not have to be raised in any certain religion to have this type. Even a system like martial arts can represent the structure they want to perfect.

What can bring out the best in this type?

Whatever way your family exemplifies virtue, they will value it and strive to do it best. The virtues that will gain their attention include, but aren't limited to, patience, kindness, humility, chastity, temperance, charity, and diligence. They enjoy the feeling that they are making the world a better place, and often they do.

Young children with a Nun or Monk type will work very hard at being good. They will listen carefully to moral stories and talk about them with deep understanding. They will talk

Family Types

openly about their beliefs, sharing what they think is the right way. They won't ask too many questions about what is right and wrong; they believe they already know. If their family has a certain faith, they will be interested in how it works and how people practice its values. Practice could include honesty, generosity, or even keeping specific eating or fasting traditions.

How can this type be a challenge?

The child with the Monk or Nun type may feel or act superior to others because she is so sure she always knows what the right thing is. It is common for most children to see life only as black or white, but the child with the Monk or Nun type never develops the ability to see gray. Things are either wrong or right, and there is little use in learning from mistakes. A child who is the Monk or Nun type believes a person should only do the right thing, and there is no excuse for anything less. Additionally, she believes she is always capable of doing just that.

A child with the Monk or Nun type has a standard that is impossible to live up to. He may find that people become wary and annoyed by his standards. Keeping long-term friendships can be challenging, because eventually someone will say or do something that is imperfect. The Monk and Nun types will have the hardest time forgiving people who have disappointed them. After all, if they can be so virtuous, why can't others?

Also, his unbending belief about himself and his own ability to be perfect will set him up for demoralization. He will try to be perfect in every way—not for you, his parents, but because he has to live up to his own standards. You can imagine how stressful it can be for this type. When he thinks he has let himself down, he will berate and punish himself. It's common to hear a parent say to him: "You're too hard on yourself."

Chapter 3: The Divine Types

Okay, so now what do I do?

As a parent, you may find yourself telling him to take it easy and try not to be so perfect. You may encourage him to let himself off the hook about some things and to be okay with making mistakes, but his very nature is in trying to be perfect. You are asking him to be less of himself, and that is impossible. In fact, he may even lose some respect for you if you advocate anything that is less than perfection. He may even become more focused on moral perfectionism to prove he's right.

The secret to having a peace between moral values and the real life experience is in the very virtues that he or she tries to emulate. I will attempt a very brief rundown of those I listed above. If you have others in your culture that your child is following, take the time to look into their meaning, not only as a literal translation, but as a symbol of balance. That way, your child will have a chance to live in balance instead of feeling never good enough.

For instance, charity or generosity is a common virtue that the Monk or Nun will try to embody. They may work hard at giving to others who are less fortunate. They may even give away their own things. The negative and extreme side of this virtue appears when they believe they shouldn't have worldly goods for themselves, and that others don't need or deserve to have plenty. When a child with the Monk or Nun type has this self-righteous viewpoint, it has gone to the extreme. It won't work to tell him he needs to be less extreme; to a child with the Monk or Nun type, more virtue is better.

Help them see that when they decide someone is greedy, or when they believe someone doesn't deserve something, they are being selfish with their approval. They aren't extending themselves generously to give that person the benefit of the doubt. A truly generous person will let others have credit,

Family Types

praise, and riches without needing proof of their worthiness.

Humility is often easy for a Monk or Nun. A Nun will be modest and not become wrapped up in vanity like other girls. The Monk may refuse to show off his talents and even say he has none. A Nun may downplay her contributions to a project, but she may get very upset when someone else is getting attention. She may even try to cause shame to that person. The saddest element of the Monk or Nun is that they will feel that they shouldn't become too valuable—that getting attention, even for good work, is the opposite of humility. To them, it is less virtuous to get attention for success or abilities. In fact, they may feel shame when they do something well and are recognized. The key is to teach them that the virtue lies in thinking of others more often, and thinking of themselves less often—not thinking less of themselves.

The kindness and compassion that Monk and Nun types give to others should be given to themselves with the same kindness. Notice how your child speaks about himself. If he doesn't describe himself with kindness, gently remind him that he is worthy of the same kindness he would give to others. In fact, it is part of his responsibility to do so.

He or she may be able to treat certain humble people with patience and mercy, but may find that some people may be unworthy of this virtue. A Monk or Nun may forget that even difficult or sinful people deserve the grace of patience. Although this is a challenge for anyone, the true virtue lies in extending patience to those for whom it is hardest to be patient. The gifts of mercy and forgiveness are truly a gift when they aren't deserved. When you share this perspective with your Monk or Nun, explain that mastering this virtue often takes a lifetime and to be patient with herself as she learns it.

Because the Monk and Nun work very hard to be good and virtuous, they may fall to sloth or laziness in other areas

Chapter 3: The Divine Types

of their life. The virtue of diligence is going to be challenging when he or she perceives certain work as too difficult because he or she has spent so much time and energy on goals that they feel were worthy. The virtue of diligence is a virtue because it's hard, boring, or of little outward value. A Monk or Nun can do things that are hard for most, and they may feel they did enough, but diligence is required for whatever is challenging to each person.

The self-righteousness of the Monk or Nun is undermining to a family unit, because the Monk or Nun will act above all others. While parents will likely support the good things their child does for others, it shouldn't give him license to skip out on the chores that all family members share.

Another virtue that is sometimes taken too far is temperance, or self-control. Often a Monk or Nun can stay cool and collected in the face of others' rage, but may use that ability to incite others. It's becoming rare today to see people keep their cool and avoid overreacting in a disagreement. On the surface, the virtue of self-control is a much-needed gift. Temperance is a refreshing alternative to outwardly expressed anger. The shadow of this virtue is when a Monk or Nun becomes self-righteous and feeds off the rage of others.

This occurs when your child passively provokes another person into a rage with a demeaning play of self-control. Modern psychology calls this passive-aggressiveness. On the outside, the Monk or Nun looks cool and level-headed, but he or she is actually belittling and provoking the frustration and rage of others. Many parents find themselves incited by the cool, laid-back attitude of their Monk or Nun. This is a dangerous pattern and must be addressed as soon as it is recognized.

If you are struggling with this as a parent it is imperative to stop the dynamic. You will never overcome the Monk or Nun's

Family Types

belief that keeping cool is always right and the only thing that's right. To try to get them to hear you when they are locked in their self-righteous belief is a complete waste of time. As with any gluttonous situation, take the food away and your Monk or Nun will have nothing to feed off of. Find a way to remove yourself from the situation immediately. Do not feed your need for satisfaction, either. Refuse to engage your child in that manner at all. Whatever the original disagreement is about is irrelevant. The disagreement must stop immediately.

This is when firm parenting must take place. Set a rule and consequence about the matter that you feel is fair. Follow through with no discussion. The pattern of losing your self-control in front of your child, and your child discovering the power he has to bring that out in you, must be stopped. There are times when trying to talk it out just doesn't work.

After your child recognizes that you've been able to follow through with your resolve on the issue and you have not gotten hotheaded, he may be able to talk with you about it in a respectful way. Never allow your child to demean you. If he is playing it cool and it drives you bananas, he has demeaned you. Don't feed that scenario ever again. If you wouldn't do that to her, she should never be allowed to do it to you.

How to be with this type:

Of all the archetypes, this one may be the trickiest. A Monk and Nun usually are smart and hardworking. They're focused and aware of all those around them. Because they are hardworking, they may expect special treatment. This could set up a challenging parent-child dynamic. Stay out of conflict if at all possible by allowing your child to learn the pitfalls of life naturally.

Although they may have frequent trials, they know they are here for a purpose. Take time to talk with your Monk or

Chapter 3: The Divine Types

Nun about his or her values. Learn how her mind thinks and what beliefs she has. When you know the places he sees things as only black and white, it will help you guide him when he's struggling with shades of gray.

Give her a structure that she can use to express these beliefs. Although traditional religion is often the venue, a Monk or Nun may find fulfillment in other places as well. Martial arts and even the healing arts, including the medical field, may be of interest to them. A Monk and Nun will love ritual. Find rituals that have meaning and help them with their purpose.

Learning how to manage the virtues they value, and even understanding the different vices, will help your Monk or Nun follow his or her deep calling without becoming self-righteous. If your child who is the Monk or Nun type is open to learning and listening to his calling, he is destined to make this world a better place. In turn, he or she will make you a very proud parent.

Martyr

**She has the strength to endure a challenging situation.
He's self-sacrificing and generous.**

Is this your child?

She will always let someone else have the first choice. She'll try to keep peace, and never rock the boat or insist on her way. She'll be easy-going and easy to please most of the time. But then there are times when she just has to have things her way, and she'll insist that she deserves it because she never gets her turn. She'll whine and cry and act as if the world owes her a chance.

What can bring out the best in this type?

If your family is ever going through a tough time or a truly challenging situation, the Martyr will be there in full support. When those around her are at their worst, she will be at her best. She's perceptive and comforting. She will be hardworking and not complain at all. She'll be your rock.

She also loves to give to others, even things that she likes for herself. She'll even give away her own things just because it feels good to do so, but sometimes she'll give and feel terrible after. If you ask her why she gave something special away, she'll say it's because the other person wanted it so much. She'll believe others want things more than she ever will.

Chapter 3: The Divine Types

How can this type be a challenge?

A Martyr believes that in order to be good and valuable, she must give and sacrifice. In other words, the more she suffers for another person, the better she is as a person. This value system is poison for anyone with the Martyr type because they have no self-worth unless they're giving. Generosity isn't healthy if the goal of giving is to make yourself feel valuable.

The child with the Martyr archetype will sacrifice her own desires very frequently, and eventually she will start a habit of complaining. First, she'll over-extend herself helping other family members who could probably help themselves. She'll believe that she can relieve them of some kind of struggle. Eventually her family members may assume that she just likes to do those things because she's so pleased to help. She'll begin to feel unappreciated and resentful. Then it's only matter of time before the "poor me" mentality kicks in.

If another family member is opinionated or strong-willed about things, the Martyr may claim she doesn't care. She won't want to make things more difficult for others, but then she isn't speaking up about her needs, either. It will make things easier, and most families will allow it to happen and even push the Martyr to give in. Family members often take the path of least resistance, but there will be a day when the Martyr has just had enough.

Because she expects others to notice what she needs, she'll assume they'll eventually give it to her. She deserves it, after all. But that almost never happens. She may get very indignant and hurt because no one is sacrificing for her like she did for them. She'll even blame her family for making her wait too long to get what she needs, even if she didn't once speak up and tell them.

For example, if your family is going through a tough few

Family Types

months financially, a Martyr won't ask for anything material. She'll go without decent shoes or other functional items in order to help the situation. But when other family members get a new pair of shoes because they needed them, the Martyr will get very upset. It may seem strange that your usually generous child is over-the-top upset about a sibling getting a needed item. Parents often feel like it came out of nowhere. What they may not realize is their child was long and silently suffering for the good of the family.

A child with the Martyr type will find ways to carry the weight of the world on their shoulders. She'll even believe she's helping her parents by worrying for them. Martyrs won't talk about how worried they are, and they won't seek to feel better, either. They think they're doing a good thing when they are "silent sufferers."

Okay, so now what do I do?

Teach your children that generosity is supposed to be fulfilling even if no one knows about it. Feeling satisfied and fulfilled with giving comes when we expect nothing in return—nothing, not even recognition. If we could help another person with an action that is invisible to them, and feel content and proud of ourselves, then we are truly generous.

Teach your children that giving and helping are wonderful, but the minute they sacrifice for others and start complaining that they should get the same treatment, do not give it to them. Don't give them a pat on the back if they complain at all. Remind them that if they want to talk about how proud or happy they feel about giving, then that is welcomed, but no one owes them anything.

A Martyr needs to learn how to ask for what she needs. Teach your children that if they help another person and need something in return, that's fine, but they need to say as much.

Chapter 3: The Divine Types

Your Martyr needs to learn how to speak up for what she needs before she gives too much. This may be surprisingly difficult, because a Martyr thinks others should just see a person's needs like she can.

If she made the assumption that others would return her care, but they don't, find out if she spoke up for herself and if she was vocal enough to be heard. Don't feed her weakness and speak up for her. She must learn to do it herself. A Martyr will be undervalued her whole life if she doesn't learn the essential skill of speaking up. Start teaching it while she's young.

How to be with this type:

Often parents feel like they should reward good behavior, especially when their child works hard to get a reward. Sadly, parents could be setting up their children for a lifetime of disappointment if their children never learn that working hard isn't always rewarded the way they expect. Although we don't want our children to be stingy, it doesn't help to teach them that when they give it must be returned to them. That's still stingy.

Remember to teach a Martyr to ask for what she needs. She's valuable as she is, and she doesn't have to be in terrible condition before her needs get met.

Children often like to give things to others, and that's beautiful, but if your child becomes sad after giving things away, then she hasn't honored herself. If this happens, don't replace the item she gave away. She needs to experience the discomfort of self-betrayal. That will help her think more carefully the next time she thinks about giving something precious away. And if she does decide to give, she'll have true satisfaction in giving.

The story of Santa Clause is an example of how to give in a healthy way. Santa doesn't give unless someone actually asks. He doesn't have to give what's asked for. He gives to those

Family Types

who deserve; he may not give anything if they don't deserve it. He gives because he just loves to give. He doesn't have to be there to see the reaction when they get the gift, and he doesn't expect a thank-you note. But if he ever gets one, it's so special. You owe him nothing, he owes you nothing, but it's lovely to experience the joy of giving and receiving. Santa doesn't work so hard he becomes cranky, but he does make every effort to making others happy. And that makes the world a better place.

Samaritan

**He's always the one to make friends
with the new kid at school.
She'll extend kindness to those who others ignore.**

Is this your child?

A Samaritan archetype, just like in the Bible, will stop to comfort someone that most people would rather avoid. In fact, the only time he may step in to help someone is when all others ignore that person. A child with the Samaritan type makes friends easily and won't exclude an underdog or outsider in his circle of companions.

What brings out the best in this type?

He will be the first to notice and comfort someone who needs it. If there is a new kid at school, and he or she is not yet incorporated into a group, a Samaritan will do something to help the new kid feel welcomed. Maybe he'll tell him or her a joke, or give the new kid a nickname like the rest of the kids. He can befriend anyone, even those who others could not. The kind of help a Samaritan gives to people is comfort and friendship, not protection or rescue.

How can this type be a challenge?

When a Samaritan gives of himself to help an outsider, he isn't going to immediately ask for a pat on the back. Deep down he feels good doing this kid of work, and at first that's enough. Eventually, though, he will crave validation for it.

When the feeling of satisfaction wears off, and the person he's helped no longer needs it, he may look for a way to extend the good feelings. One common method is making the outsider act grateful for the help long after it's appropriate. The Samaritan may start to use tactics like reminding the outsider that he was there for him or her. He may even nudge the outsider into saying "thank you" again and again.

Okay, so now what do I do?

While encouragement and love from others are always part of a full healthy life, we don't want our children to grow into needy people who can never feel satisfied. Our children need to learn how to be able to give themselves recognition and feel satisfied without the help of others. This won't happen overnight, so parents will have to be the first people to validate the good works of their children. Parents can let the Samaritan know that they notice how kind he is and that they are very proud of him. Most of the things people believe about themselves as adults are things that their parents told them when they were young.

When we spend a healthy amount of time telling our children that we notice the wonderful things they do and the wonderful people that they are, they will grow to have that image of themselves.

But this must also be balanced by teaching the child how to listen to his own inner voice of validation. Parents could ask the child what he thinks of how he's done and suggest he listen to that opinion as well. Eventually, when the child reaches his teenage years, he could be only asked about his opinion instead of being given his parents'.

If your child has the Samaritan archetype it is essential to make the time and take the effort to give him validation and recognition. That needs to be followed by lessons on how to listen to his inner voice and make that the most important of all. After they have grown and leave the nest, both his parents' words and his own will resound in his ears and fuel a sense of worthiness that needs no audience to confirm.

How to be with this type:

Our kids don't need to be on display or shouted about to everyone about how great they are. Take a quiet moment every so often to talk to them. Remind them of their gifts, like making others feel cared for, and that you noticed. That can be one of the sweetest moments of parenthood for us, and a deeply fulfilling moment as a child.

Priest

**He's a good listener and brings wisdom to others.
He's ahead of his time, wise, and trustworthy.**

Is this your child?

A child with the Priest type may never actually become a priest. What he will have is a strong desire to help others. More specifically, he will bring comfort and even wisdom to others. He will end up as a trusted listener to others, particularly in matters of the heart or issues of moral and value judgments.

The child the Priest type will enjoy taking a leadership role in his family's spiritual or religious practice. He may frequently volunteer to say the blessing over the meal. He may offer to help siblings study and prepare for their religious education. He will look for ways to serve whatever spiritual practice you follow.

What can bring out the best in this type?

A child with the Priest type feels the need to take responsibility for others and will feel honored when it's given to him. He's most happy to help in some way. As long as he knows he's benefiting others, he'll be content.

He'll notice when others need a supportive and understanding ear. He's a good listener. He may even seem older than his age because he is wise in his understanding of

Chapter 3: The Divine Types

the problems people share. He also has a huge capacity to empathize with and comfort people.

How can this type be a challenge?

Because a child with the Priest type is naturally responsible, he will likely be trusted by others. This is a healthy and natural progression, but if your child isn't yet ready to handle that trust, he may make some naïve mistakes. It's exciting for an adolescent to gain some respect and trust from others. If his friends or even adults feel that they can confide in him, he may not yet have the skills to know when he should or should not tell others. It's often in these tender years that he will become full of himself and say things about people that he should keep private.

A common mistake for a child with the Priest type is talking about the private matters of others, particularly matters that were supposed to be in confidence. Further, if your child has had experiences when he was trusted with personal information, then didn't keep it to himself, it is a sign that he needs help for the next step in development. The child with the Priest type needs to have support as he takes on issues that other people share with him. It's inevitable for this type to need a mentor or guide to help him learn to manage the responsibility.

Okay, so now what do I do?

A child with the Priest archetype may not seek support for himself because he may feel he should only help others, but support is exactly what he needs. If he makes the mistake of telling the personal secrets of others when it's not appropriate, it's a strong indication that he needs to talk about what he's experiencing with someone. He needs a friend or mentor to listen to him so he's not left to handle it on his own. The friend or mentor can be a parent, relative, or anyone who can empathize and understand the importance of the issues that are coming up. It's also necessary for the friend or mentor to keep the information confidential. People will trust a child with the Priest type with private information, and his support should be trustworthy as well.

Parents shouldn't underestimate how helpful the child with the Priest type can be to others. This type is a great salve to many children who may not have the kind of friendships that can handle sharing difficult private information. Like the quote "A problem shared is a problem divided," the child with the Priest type is an important part of our society. We should all be so lucky as to have this kind of friend.

It's also important to decipher the difference between your child listening to gossip, becoming someone's therapist, and actually finding himself in situations where he can share some wisdom. If he sounds like he is helping others, and you can tell he is feeling positive about his role, then he is likely doing good things with his ability.

But if he's listening to people backstab or trash-talk others, and then passing on the gossip as well, he may not be a Priest type but a Gossip type. Additionally, if he's the kind of person to give advice to people even if they don't ask, he may be a Rescuer type.

How to be with this type:

Sometimes parents get nervous if their young son or daughter is listening to others talk about issues that are serious. We want to keep our children innocent. But if your child has the Priest type, and can comfort others with wisdom and even prayer, then he has an important role to fulfill in his life. Many people will be soothed and nourished by his care. If he begins to "blab" about the private matters that were shared with him, it means he also needs someone to talk to. It's not

Chapter 3: The Divine Types

a sign that something is going wrong, but a sign of growth.

Our job as parents is to make sure our children have a healthy and safe place in which to share their experiences. Children need to know they're not alone. If there is an issue that is truly out of their league, they need to have a good advisor to help them.

If you can identify the Priest as an archetype of your child, you will likely be very proud of him. With the right support he can bring wisdom and comfort to many people, and find fulfillment in his calling.

Angel

**She loves to help others and never wants anything in return.
She can bring out the best in us.**

Is this your child?

There are many kinds of Angels: the protector Angel, the quiet-helpful Angel, and even the gift Angel who challenges us to handle her with care and tenderness. Whether she's protecting, helping, or challenging someone, all Angel types have a common purpose to bring out the best in us.

A child with the Angel type is usually gentle in her nature. She will also inspire others to treat her gently. She will be sensitive and particularly empathetic. As a baby she'll react strongly to times when her parents are upset. Parents may learn very quickly to keep their emotions under control around this child, and in the long run that could be good. This could be difficult for parents who are not naturally quiet and gentle.

Parents of children with a physical or mental disability sometimes call their child their "angel." This is another way a child can have an Angel type. Parents who have to deal with the requirements of disabled or sick children may find that they must exercise tremendous patience and endurance. In this way the Angel child is bringing out the best in them.

Chapter 3: The Divine Types

What brings out the best in this type?

A child with the Angel type will thrive on trying to make things right. She will work very hard at changing something that she thinks is unfair. She may become very adamant about stopping an injustice and then work to make it right.

The child with the Angel type will love to help others, and often doesn't want attention or a reward. She may even sneak and help others, so no one knows what good she did. She'll notice when something isn't fair and often try to do something to make it right. She may seem nosy, especially when there is an injustice.

For parents who have a mentally or physically disabled Angel child, learning to appreciate life's small but important successes can be easier. The perspective that is gained from enduring the hardships and challenges of everyday life can bring peace and wisdom that few can hope for.

How can this type be a challenge?

An Angel may be judgmental of others, always thinking she knows better. She may be overprotective and over-empathetic, and take on too much worry for others. Movies and stories that have a "dark angel" figure show how an Angel type can go too far to balance the scales of justice. For example, Batman was a dark angel. The Angel type uses good to fight evil, but often there is a self-sacrificing part of the character that ends up going too far.

A child with an Angel may go to extremes to do what's good. For example, she may become the only vegetarian in her family because she saw a documentary about cruelty to animals. In the family unit, this type can be a challenge because, once the Angel decides what's right, she must follow that decision. As a

Family Types

parent, you may find yourself trying to teach your Angel to see things with balance and perspective.

A child who is disabled is a challenge if only because of the often grueling and exhausting work it takes to care for her. When parents are faced with the challenge day in and day out, inevitably they will become stronger and more patient if they strive to execute the job with love and tenderness. While there can be no full explanation for why some of us have this kind of challenge with our children, there is no doubt a purpose that comes with it. Raising a child with a disability is work that can hone and polish us to be our best.

Okay, so now what do I do?

When the child with the Angel type has gone to extremes to balance the scales of justice and deny herself some of the good things in life, it can be hard for parents to just watch. As adults, we know that extreme behavior changes in one person, in an effort to make a global change, is usually not worth it. It can be hard to watch our child refuse some of the good things in life because she thinks it will change others. But what looks like a sacrifice to our child may not actually feel like one to him or her.

In fact, a child with an Angel type feels very empowered when she is making a huge sacrifice. It would be wise for parents to set aside their worries, and when possible let the Angel child learn the discipline and dedication it takes to follow through.

The only time we should put a stop to our Angel is when it is detrimental to her health or well-being, or when the entire family suffers from the commitment to change. But if parents are in the position of constantly talking their child down from extreme self-righteous behavior, it may mean it's time to dig in to what she believes.

There are two reasons an Angel decides to go to extremes to change the world. The first is that she is very sensitive

Chapter 3: The Divine Types

and has very strong feelings, especially when she experiences something unfair. The second is that the Angel type needs to make things right. People without this type may see something unfair and talk about it or even rant about it. But a child with the Angel type must go further—much further—and that's where parenting can become so difficult.

Often children think in terms of black or white, and have no idea that there are gray areas, or even debatable areas. It could help to take the time, and it may be a lot, to sit and listen to the child, and take in all of her beliefs. Parents can gently ask where she heard or learned her facts to understand what she believes. Then doing a search with your child to find out if all the facts are indeed true will help get each of you on the same page.

Sometimes things aren't as dire as she believed. Sometimes, though, they are, and it would be important for parents to help her find a balanced way to act on the issue.

One immensely important method is searching to see who is already doing things to make the wrong right. An Angel feels singularly responsible to change the world, but if parents can show her that many others are already working on the problem and finding success, then it will calm her worry and drive.

How to be with this type:

The Angel type can be a great help at home, especially if she knows she's making your life better. Although she may go to extremes to make something change, her intentions are pure and well-meaning. She needs someone to listen to and understand her deep desire to make the world better. She also needs someone to guide her to find all the facts so she can keep an open mind. She needs to know that others are like her and are already helping make things better. Your guardian Angel feels as though she has a big job. It helps her to know she's not alone and that her parents understand.

Chapter 4
The Wisdom Types

Teacher

Student

Seeker

Hermit

Storyteller

Judge

The Wisdom archetypes represent the kind of children who seem to know more than their peers. They are not necessarily smarter, but they understand human nature better than others and often say things that are surprising for their age. They don't usually hold back their opinion, and there is usually some truth in what they say.

They have abilities to deal with people in difficult situations. Their opinions are often in black-and-white terms, but they deserve our attention because they remind us of the truth. As parents we often teach our children right from wrong, but we don't always follow our own rules. For example, we tell them not to yell at each other, but we yell at them when we feel it's necessary. A child with a Wisdom type may point it out to us.

Often kids today speak their thoughts without censorship to parents and other adults. It is not necessarily a Wisdom type trying to share what he or she knows. It could just be a phase of learning to speak up for themselves. Are they critical or actually sharing an observation? Criticism is not wisdom.

A child with one of these types may use a teaching method to convey wise information. He could be the classic Teacher type or Storyteller type. A Judge type is able to see both sides of an issue and still determine that one is more valid than the other. Sometimes a child will search out wisdom by learning or even taking quiet reflection time as in the Student, Seeker, or Hermit type.

Any of these types can be either a boy or girl, and the gender I have chosen is for simplicity in reading, not an indication of male or female.

Family Types

If your child said something that leaves you thinking: "Ah, out of the mouth of babes" because it is profound, take note whether he or she does it often. If so, you may have a child with a Wisdom type.

Teacher

She has the ability to share what she's learned, helping others to understand.

Is this your child?

Little girls love to play "teacher." It's a phase many girls go through, but for some the phase never ends. She may use her toys or friends as students, and arrange them like a classroom. When she's learned something interesting, you'll see her try to teach anyone who will sit and listen. She's not bossy about it, but eager to share—sometimes so eager, she won't notice when others don't have the same excitement. It can wear out her friends and family. People may call her a know-it-all.

If a boy has a Teacher type, it may not show up as early or in the same way as a girl. For a boy, he may be a good student, enjoying school and learning. He will be very engaged in the classroom, and attentive to the teacher. If your son likes to raise his hand to tell the teacher some added information, even when the teacher hasn't asked, he may have a Teacher type.

What brings out the best in this type?

A girl likes to know she can help people by giving them information they don't know yet. She likes to be in charge, but only when there's information to share. She's an information leader. For example, if there are cookies to be made, she'll tell you all about what makes a good dough and the secrets to

Family Types

baking them just right. She won't take over and tell people what to do unless she's also a Queen type. A pure Teacher archetype wants to share her knowledge. If she's with someone wiser than her, she'll soak up anything she can that will add to her own knowledge base.

A boy with the Teacher type likes to be called on in class to answer questions. He feels great when the teacher, scout leader, or coach calls on him to share information. If he is proficient at something he'll have a hard time containing it. He's a pleasure to have at school because he's curious and attentive. He may bring in outside material to share on the given topic. Even if this only happens in a few classes, and he must share what he's learned, it is the seed of the Teacher.

How can this type be a challenge?

A girl may make her friends weary from all the teaching. Because she is so excited about what she's learned, she often can't imagine that others aren't as thrilled. If you see her playing "teacher" often, and her friends begin to insist on another form of play, she probably needs a little guidance from a well-meaning and informed parent. She may not be able to see why others don't feel like she does. Good teachers have strong focus and drive, which will help in a classroom of many students. But as a little girl playing with friends, it may be necessary to redirect her.

If a boy has been given a few too many chances to call out answers, he may not know when to stop. A boy could end up interrupting a teacher, constantly raising his hand, or calling out answers. He may get the reputation as a know-it-all and alienate his friends. In our competitive society, parents often don't want a child to play dumb just to fit in, but there is a time and place for speaking out. A boy who feels like he knows so much, and should share it if he thinks it helps, is out of his

Chapter 4: The Wisdom Types

league and in danger for ridicule or even a sharp response from a beloved teacher.

Okay, so now what do I do?

If a girl has a strong Teacher type, and her parents have surrounded her with materials and situations that have indulged her desire to teach, it will become a huge part of her life. As with anything that we take too far, she may begin to think that teaching others is the only thing that's fun. If you suggest another kind of play and she just can't accept that it would be fun, she may be too wrapped up in it. Take her aside, outside of her normal venue, and talk about other things that are fun for her. Plan ahead to have at least five other things you know she loves to do. Offer her specific times she can play "teacher" so she knows the boundaries. Then offer to help her set up another kind of play.

Boys who get into the Teacher type too much will have to work on their self-control. They're excited and so happy to share, but they have to allow the true teacher to do his or her job. If it's gotten to the point that he's disrupting the class, he absolutely needs a venue to let it out. Just telling him to be quiet in class will squelch the passion and joy of learning that's in him. Always reinforce that you understand he needs to share what he knows and that you will help him find a way to do that. An example may be for him to teach you or a sibling how to do something at home.

How to be with this type:

There are many places children can share a passion for teaching. Boys who join the Boy Scouts may find that younger ranks love to learn from their experience. Some schools offer tutoring to younger students by older students. That would be a prime venue for him to express himself. With a little creativity

Family Types

and research, parents may find that their child can truly help others well before he graduates from school. Kids are doing things much earlier than ever, and we all can benefit.

It's especially true to find a venue if your little Teacher can't put her attention on much else. But if she is truly too young to teach others, turn to the learning part of teaching. Children with the teacher love to learn. Find new and exciting information that branches off of what she already loves. She has a huge appetite for learning, and it can be such a pleasure to feed it. It time, she will return to others what she's learned.

Student

**He's bright and intelligent.
He loves to learn, and he's curious about many topics.**

Is this your child?

A child with the Student type will love the process of learning and building knowledge. He will probably love books, computers, and educational shows. Often he will enjoy school so much that when he grows up he will feel most at home in a classroom and become a teacher. He may ask a lot of questions, and even though he may know more about some subjects than others, he may never feel like he's learned enough.

What brings out the best in this type?

Any learning environment will bring out the best in him. He may not love all subjects and may not even get the best grades, but he'll make school look easy. He'll like to just sit back and soak up the knowledge. He'll often share all the interesting things he learned at school. If you take him to museums he'll be content and absorbed for hours.

Usually a child with the Student type has a specialty. Perhaps he is a student of the arts. No matter what you bring him (the theater, art museums, or craft shows), he'll take all of it in. If your Student loves history, he'll find those venues to be exciting and fun. Having a child who shares similar interests to

Family Types

you is wonderful, but it's even better if he has the unquenchable thirst of a Student.

How can this type be a challenge?

As a parent of a child with the Student type, you will have it easy with schoolwork, accept when your Student thinks he knows it all. He may fail to study enough for tests and underestimate the material, because learning is easy and he can absorb so much so quickly. Parents may think their child is lazy because he's smart enough to have better grades. The "laziness" comes from the belief that learning is easy and test-taking should be easy, too. Often a child with the Student type assumes learning and test-taking are the same. They're not.

As Students mature and learn the skill of taking tests, they may fall into another trap: They may think that because they've learned about something and can pass every test about it, they are now experts on the subject. Without the hands-on experience it takes to be a true expert, they may again underestimate what is needed. It's like learning about driving a car from a book, taking the test that gives them a permit, and then claiming to know how to actually drive. They haven't yet gotten behind the wheel to experience it, but think it's easy.

Any number of situations can become a tug-o-war between parents and Students. The child with the Student type doesn't realize how hard something is, and the parent can see the child getting in over his head. The parent has heard "I already know that" for the thousandth time, and even "Leave me alone, it's not that hard," but sometimes it *is* that hard.

Okay, so now what do I do?

Forcing them to admit they don't know enough is going to set the parent up for a face-off. To avoid this, first, the parent could just ignore the arrogance and pretend not didn't hear them. It

Chapter 4: The Wisdom Types

really doesn't matter that the Student is puffed up and ready to show off. Telling him he's wrong backs him into a corner.

Instead, the parent could decide if it's worth the trouble to let the child make the mistake. It's not worth it if there is danger or extreme waste that will come of it. But if the child is capable of making the mistake, and cleaning or fixing the ensuing mess, it could definitely be worth it.

It's like letting steam off that's bottled up in a pressure cooker. The child is allowed to try something too difficult and make a mess or mistake. Without any fuss from his parent, except that he must clean it up, he'll be all the wiser the next time he pushes to try something too hard. When the time comes for the parent to put her foot down, he'll know he's trusted to try things but that this is not one of those times.

It may sound opposite to what we believe, but setting up a system that puts the child in control of as much as possible, as soon as possible, means he'll learn responsibility.

If a book-smart Student type reads a cookbook and wants to make dinner all by himself, it may seem like too much effort for the parent to stand by, guide, and watch. The more the child is trusted to do, though, the more he'll understand how difficult a job really is. That perspective can only be learned with experience, and because the parent doesn't fuss about the mess, but insists the child clean up, the child will also become proud of his capabilities and develop healthy self-esteem.

There is a secret to knowing when we need to give our children the chance to experience what they've learned in a book. The secret is in his arrogance. In other words, the more he claims to know enough, the more parents should give him the chance to try and take responsibility for the outcome.

Without this life experience, there is a sad pitfall that many Students experience once they're adults. If we don't give them hands-on experience and help them build the endurance to clean up after a mess, we will undermine their belief in their own ability.

How many times have we met someone who is so smart and knows so much, but sadly doesn't do much with it? Could it be that this person was protected from his or her own curiosity and the inevitable mistakes and messes?

It's not possible to be born with intense curiosity like the Student type and have no interest in experiencing it. Adults who can't or don't take their book knowledge and find a way to experience it out in the world have lost a belief in themselves. These adults were smart, curious children. Did their parents squelch the next step in their development?

How to be with this type:

The Student type should experience the difference between mental knowledge and actually doing things as often as possible. The ability to work at something and truly become proficient can't be taught with lectures or by just reading about it. The Student must experience over and over the effort it takes to succeed. A parent can never just model this. A parent must let him fail while trying.

Obviously as parents we have to make sure our know-it-all is safe. Sometimes the answer is "No, you're just not ready. It's too risky to let you do that." Feeding the Student's curiosity when possible will help balance the times when the parents simply cannot allow it.

By far, the most important job of a parent is to reinforce our belief in our children. When a Student feels confident, he will learn to use his talents in a constructive way. The most effective tool for a parent who has a child with a Student type is teaching him how to carry the knowledge he's learned into action he can experience.

Seeker

**She is curious about truth and wisdom.
She has the ability to understand universal wisdom from many different sources.**

Is this your child?

She's wise for her age. A child with the Seeker type will listen to the advice of elders and people with more experience. She can understand certain universal truths quicker and in more depth than others her age. She may be curious about how people have made mistakes and what lessons came from that. With this knowledge, she can learn from others' mistakes and avoid making them herself.

A Seeker may have an interest in a specific facet of life. For example, if she loves science she'll spend vast time and energy trying to figure out how life works at its core. If she is interested in the way things are constructed, she'll seek to learn how things are put together and what makes one better than another. If she's interested in the human condition, she may look for the best way to be in a relationship.

What brings out the best in this type?

Parents of a Seeker may be proud of how grounded and self-assured she seems, even trusting her to make sound judgments earlier than others her age. She'll be a good listener

Family Types

and attentive to rules that are presented as wise. She won't like making naïve mistakes.

The Seeker is hungry for more. She will be fascinated with learning what's right and wrong. She'll ask questions and easily understand complex issues. She'll enjoy conversations about how the world works and what's good and bad.

She'll love reading about people who have overcome adversity, and even become inspired by them. To the child with the Seeker type, it's exciting to learn how to change a bad situation into a good one. Girl Seekers may be curious about romantic wisdom and how to find true love. Boys may wish to learn what knowledge will give them power over others.

How can this type be a challenge?

In the Wisdom category, many of the archetypes have a common thread. The Seeker, like several others, believes that she knows better than others. Because she has learned things that seem important, and other children have not yet learned them, the child with the Seeker type can become self-righteous, and no one likes a self-righteous person.

Also, the Seeker may have a habit of talking with authority on an issue, but then she learns another point of view and switches her belief. While it's fine to have a change of mind when new understanding is presented, the Seeker tends to be over-zealous about an issue and can end up looking like a fool. For a parent, it can just be annoying. One day she's sure she knows it all and she's insistent that everyone in the family agrees with her. The next week she's seen the other side of the issue and now everyone else should be, too. She can be intolerant of people who seem naïve to her.

Okay, so now what do I do?

What a Seeker struggles with is acceptance for others who

don't seem to share the same wisdom. What a Seeker needs to learn is that others will arrive to understanding in their own way, and that's a good thing. What a parent can do is teach this essential piece of wisdom.

While we never want to squelch the thirst and desire for learning, our Seeker child needs to learn the wisdom of allowing others their own experience and opinions. Help your Seeker understand that if she thinks that everyone should agree about something, then they won't have the chance to decide for themselves.

Another method of taming the pushiness of a Seeker is to make time to listen to her. Often the Seeker will soak up what people believe, but without the chance to process those thoughts, and share those thoughts, she can become forceful. She may just need some one-on-one time to talk about what she thinks. Children who do a lot of thinking and processing need an audience to bounce their thoughts off of. As parents, we can make a huge impact on our children's disposition by taking time to listen to them.

How to be with this type:

Although a Seeker may seem conceited and intolerant at times, she will also work hard to make intelligent choices. She may often think she has all the answers, and this will likely get worse as she becomes a teenager. Parents may laugh to themselves, knowing life's pitfalls will take care of her misconceptions. As a parent of a Seeker, we have it pretty easy.

When she becomes too pushy with her beliefs, it may mean that it's time to spend some time listening to her ideas and beliefs. Sometimes a little extra attention is all that's needed to tame the difficult side of this type. What is left is a smart and wise child that is ahead of her time.

Hermit

**He needs time to be left alone.
He is private and thoughtful.**

Is this your child?

He's happy to play by himself and doesn't ask to have friends over. Although he's willing to play with others, he needs a period of time to be alone. On vacations he can get exhausted and overwhelmed if he can't have time alone for a few days. Parents of a Hermit type often already know if their child is the kind who just needs to be left alone regularly.

He can be shy and uncomfortable around new people. When people are visiting his home, he may stay in his room alone until he's told to come out and join the rest. He can socialize for a while, but will retreat to a quiet place if he can.

What brings out the best in this type?

If a child with the Hermit type is lucky enough to have his own room he'll be content. If he must share a room, he will want a place to get away from people. It could be outside or in an unused area of the house.

He's better when he's one-on-one with people. He may enjoy conversation and visiting with a small number of close family or friends, but he'll have to work at socializing in large groups. He may wish he liked big parties, but he's just not as comfortable with them.

Chapter 4: The Wisdom Types

A child with the Hermit type can be very creative. Usually he will enjoy reading, drawing, writing, building, or some kind of creative play. A child who just wants to play video games all day is not necessarily a Hermit. If the child needed quiet time every day since he was a baby, he would likely have this type. It would not surprise a parent of a Hermit type if he had said, "Leave me alone," at 12 years old. He had probably been saying it since he was 2.

How can this type be a challenge?

Because a child with the Hermit type will not want to socialize very often, it can be a challenge for a busy family to cut back on their activities. It can become a tug-o-war when one child is resistant to going out or visiting, and the rest are excited to leave. It may be almost impossible to balance this issue at times, and everyone could end up feeling like they can't have their way.

If the family pushes too often to take the Hermit out of his comfort zone, he can become overwhelmed if he's too stimulated by crowds and activity. His behavior can range from temper tantrums in public to crying easily to aggressive behavior. Often parents think he may grow out of it. But even as he develops friendships he may not want to go out more. For a child with the Hermit type, the desire to socialize won't blossom like it does in other children.

Okay, so now what do I do?

If it always feels like the parents are giving in and staying home, or the child ends up having a meltdown when out socializing, then the parents are held hostage to the temperament of the child. No one wants to spend years stuck at home just to keep their child from having a fit.

The first goal of the parents should be to make sure the

Family Types

child with a Hermit type actually has a place to call his own with daily time to spend there. If he can't have his own room, a parent can help him find a place where he feels comfortable to retreat to, like a quiet corner or a space that was otherwise saved for storage. It may seem unfair to other siblings that they don't get their own space, but it's worth the experiment to see if the whole family can get along better. If he has time alone enough, it may free everyone to get out more.

Sometimes a child with the Hermit type seems to get worse when the seasons are at their extreme, as in the dead of winter or during the heat of summer. This may be because he can't get outside regularly and that's been his place to become more calm and centered. If this is true, he would need a place to retreat to only during those months.

The next goal of the parent could be to protect this time and make sure siblings or noises don't invade the space. If the child is always feeling like his space is a little invaded, he'll be even more intolerant of getting out into the world. It's not necessary to have perfect silence unless your child is extremely sensitive, but take notice if the child seems more calm and social if he has had a very peaceful retreat.

Once the child with the Hermit type has filled his need for silence and privacy he may still ask for more, but he'll likely be more willing to go out and interact with others. It should take less nudging, and he should be able to last longer, which will help balance the family dynamic.

How to be with this type:

The Hermit can be misunderstood, and the parent/child relationship can turn into a frustrating tug-o-war. Often parents try to give the child what he wants, and it just doesn't seem like he'll ever come out of his shell. When we can tell our Hermit child that we understand and honor his need for privacy, then

Chapter 4: The Wisdom Types

take steps to find out what kind of quality that privacy should be, we are well on our way to helping our Hermit feel less pressed and pushed. Over time, he should feel a sense of calm because he is really able to fill his need. Once his deepest need is fed, he should begin to share more of himself with others.

Storyteller

**He uses stories to share what he's learned.
He loves to engage people in listening to a tale.**

Is this your child?

There's no short answer with this type. If you ask how his day was after school he'll go on and on about the day's events. After he's seen an entertaining TV show he'll want to tell you what happened, blow-by-blow. He loves people to listen to him, but he also loves to listen to someone else tell a great story. If you tell him you have a story to share, you'll have his attention every time.

What brings out the best in this type?

Eye contact and a good, listening ear will bring out the best in him. It can take patience, but when he wants to share a story it's worth it to put down what you're doing and listen. He may take a long time to get to the point, but each time he has an audience to tell his stories to he's developing his own style. A good storyteller needs practice, and to get practice he needs an audience.

If you have a lesson to teach him about a subject that seems preachy, he'll respond well to it delivered in a story. For example, if parents want him to clean his room they can begin with "Let me tell you about the boy who never cleaned up his room." You'll have his attention captured, and maybe he'll even clean his room without complaint.

Chapter 4: The Wisdom Types

How can this type be a challenge?

If we are too busy too often to take the time to listen to our Storyteller, he may start to embellish his stories to get more attention. From there, he may form a habit of stretching the truth and even lying. The parents of a Storyteller shouldn't be worried that it's our job alone to prevent this. The Storyteller has a tendency to change the facts just because it makes the story better, but this issue can become a lifetime habit if we aren't aware of it.

If we start to wonder if the stories are true every time we hear "Guess what happened today?" then we may need to have a talk with our Storyteller about the difference between a story and relating facts. Children can get wrapped up in a method of getting attention and truly forget how to tell the truth.

Okay, so now what do I do?

Most Storytellers who fall into this trap are too young to understand all the consequences of what they are saying. It may take a few lectures and even repeating the classic "The Boy Who Cried Wolf" story to get the point across. If we can guide him while he's young and help him decipher the times when he must be accurate, he'll be less likely to make embellishment a habit.

How to be with this type:

The child with the Storyteller type is fun and entertaining. Any family is lucky to have one. It's a joy to have a child desire to share his imagination with others, and we would be wise to slow down and listen. Except for the likely period of teaching them when only facts are acceptable, this type could keep us engaged and inspired with their stories for the rest of our lives.

Judge

She likes to hear both sides of a disagreement so she can determine who is right.

Is this your child?

She'll give you her opinion even if you haven't asked. She believes she knows what's right even if she's very young. She'll love to solve problems particularly if she can decide between one choice and another. She isn't as interested in helping people work together try to figure out a mutual agreement as much as deciding if one is right and the other wrong.

What brings out the best in this type?

The child with the Judge type won't sit by and let her friends argue. She's a problem-solver, and she's driven to get people to stop their disagreements. She'll try to be fair and hear out both sides, but when she thinks she's heard enough she'll decide that only one side can win and that's the way it will be.

The best part of the Judge is that she's not wishy-washy. This type can make a decision and feel confident in it. It can be funny to watch the determination of a young child with the Judge type. Often even adults will respect her firm decisions.

How can this type be a challenge?

Often there is no middle ground with a Judge, and her decisions can cause other children to feel unfairly treated.

Chapter 4: The Wisdom Types

Because she has a strong personality, other children may be put off. She may even have a tendency to bully those who she knows will back down to her decisions.

For example, if a group of friends is having a hard time sharing a toy, like a jump rope, the child with the Judge type will tell them who will take a turn and when. Maybe no one had asked her, and they were struggling to do it without her, but she will demand that they do it her way. She will believe she's helping them, and she'll really think she's being fair. Perhaps she is being fair, but when other children don't want to be told what to do, they'll likely ignore her and she may feel rejected. If a child has the Judge type, she will inevitably experience hurt feelings and rejection. As her parent, it can be hard to watch.

Okay, so now what do I do?

Sometimes life's growing pains only need an empathetic parent to listen and understand. Parents could try to instill in their children that, although they are trying to help others, sometimes people want to figure things out by themselves, and it's better to let them. Most adolescents won't understand this. It may be helpful to remember a time when the child wanted to do something herself and her parents needed to do it for her. It can help her understand the way others feel when she jumps in too soon to help.

Another guiding principle is to teach a child with the Judge type that it's better to wait until people ask for help instead of assuming they want it. Even if she knows better and can solve it quicker, it's better to wait.

A child with the Judge type may take a lifetime to learn these principles. Many can grow into bossy, frustrated adults because they still think they know what's right for others, but others won't listen. If her parents can help her practice a few wise choices, she will have a much easier time keeping her friends.

Family Types

How to be with this type:

The decision skills a Judge is born with are impressive. It is wise to put her in charge when those skills will be helpful to everyone. With positive experiences she'll grow into a wise decision-maker. Help her learn when she should step in and when she shouldn't. Once she knows that sometimes she should keep her opinions to herself, it will help her manage her relationships better. She'll still make mistakes, but it's easier to get over if she can understand she needs to respect the choices of others.

She may become a complainer when no one is listening to her, so it's helpful for parents to take time to listen to her opinions whenever possible. If the child with the Judge type has a receptive and understanding parent, she will have less need to boss around others. Parents don't need to agree with their child, but understanding and acknowledging her opinions will teach her that, even in disagreement, people can get along fine.

Chapter 5
The Healing Types

Healer

Rescuer

Companion/BFF

Guide/Mentor

In the Healing category the children who have these types have a desire to help people feel better. They may help people who are frustrated and stuck with a problem, or those who have emotional pain and sadness. If they see someone suffering, they are driven to try to help them feel better. The child with one of the Healing types is often very sensitive to others and will take notice when someone is in distress. This may also include concern for animals.

These types are either male or female. I have chosen a gender only to make the writing easier to read. While reading through the Healing types, you'll see that each one is capable of creating positive relationships that can really make a difference in someone's life. No action is too small or insignificant with these types.

There are several ways that someone can heal another. While we initially think of someone who is sick, it is also healing to be rescued from a distressful situation. Therefore the Rescuer falls into this category as well.

For those who are lonely, there is a terrific healing when a companion enters the picture. As the saying goes, "A problem shared is a problem divided." Friendship is a healer.

For those of us who are lost or confused, the Guide is the perfect salve for worry and stress. The children who have a Healer type are born with a mission and purpose to take the struggle and suffering of others and turn them into healing. We are lucky to be their parents.

Healer

**She will find a way to help someone feel better.
She is sensitive and empathetic.**

Is this your child?

She may be more sensitive to pain than other children and cry easily. She has tremendous empathy when other people are upset or hurting, and she will try to help them. She has a big heart and seems to know what to do and say to help someone feel better.

As a baby she may have been easily unnerved by others who were upset. Although she needed extra care and attention, she will grow to be able to give that care back to others. If a parent notices that her child often helps others, particularly those who are sad or hurt, she may have the Healer type.

What brings out the best in this type?

The Healer type may look only like an oversensitive child who needs a lot of attention because she will have that propensity, but a sensitive child may grow to have compassion for others because she can "feel their pain." Her ability to empathize with others is strong. If she is given gentle and consistent care she will learn to treat others in the same way. Even a child as old as 2 or 3 can reach out to give hugs to a sad parent or sibling. Although it seems natural for a child with the Healer type, not all children will develop this way of caring.

Family Types

The child with the Healer type will come to life when someone is down. She won't ignore someone she thinks she can comfort. If a friend is sad she'll do anything to help her friend feel better. If she knows someone is sick, she may want to cook or pray for that person, or she may want to call or visit. She'll have a strong desire to do something.

Although many children naturally want to comfort another person, a child with the Healer type will end up finding those in need more frequently than most. She'll be the first to hear about a sick friend. She'll be the one to find a hurt animal. She'll also think about those who are not well and feel obligated to help in some way.

How can this type be a challenge?

A child with the Healer will have a propensity to help too many people at the cost of her own health. She may get involved with her friends' issues and dramas, and become exhausted and worn out from trying to support them. It is hard for a Healer to stay balanced and keep her own needs as her first priority.

Most girls have issues with getting involved with her friends' drama at some point in their life, but a girl with the Healer type will have always tried to help people and a tendency to take "helping" too far. It's a challenge as a parent to calm the concerned child down because she's trying to save someone over and over again.

Okay, so now what do I do?

The child with the Healer type will always feel tremendous responsibility for the well-being of other people. Although it's wonderful to have the talent and ability to help others feel better, it's important to learn when, where, and how much care is healthy for the Healer, too. Often children feel invincible and are willing to completely throw themselves at a problem

Chapter 5: The Healing Types

in order to solve it. So, telling the Healer that she is doing too much will likely fall on deaf ears.

The Healer type will only be concerned for the person she wants to help. Teach the Healer that it's her responsibility to model balanced behavior so that others can learn how to live better from her example. Find out what her cues are for fatigue and exhaustion, and teach her that if she can avoid those issues, she's actually a better friend.

For example, if the Healer can't get her homework done, or has a hard time sleeping because of worry, she is now the one who needs help. If all her fun time is spent comforting others, how will others learn to comfort themselves? It's an important skill for all of us. Is there time set aside for the child with the Healer type to have fun so she can refuel and feel her best? Healers take themselves very seriously, and parents would be smart to work within that mentality instead of telling them not to.

How to be with this type:

Whether it's a boy or a girl, the child with the Healer type will be a blessing to the planet. Although the parent of a Healer will have to be patient and wise in guiding their child, it could be a wonderful adventure to see her grow into a loving and giving person. Making sure the Healer doesn't get exhausted or worn out from giving too much will be a full-time job sometimes. It's an inevitable experience for most children with this type. With guidance and support from her parents, the Healer can learn first how to take care of herself, and then give to others.

Rescuer

He'll notice when someone is in trouble or distress, and offer help and support until they are safe.

Is this your child?

A child with the Rescuer type will help those who are in trouble or unfairly treated. He'll speak up for those who can't speak for themselves. If someone can't defend himself, he may stand up to a bully for that person. If he gets into fights, it's often because he's helping someone else. A child with the Rescuer type may also become involved in other people's personal problems in an effort to remedy a situation.

The Rescuer may have experiences of being bullied, and those experiences may develop his desire to protect others from going through it as well. He is very concerned about things that are unfair, especially if someone is hurt from it either emotionally or physically. His concern can be for people or animals. The Rescuer type is known to bring home lost, stray animals.

What brings out the best in this type?

The best part of the Rescuer is his ability to have courage in a difficult situation. The Rescuer jumps in where most people would fear to take a stand. The Liberator and Advocate are variations of this type. All are similar, but there are a few differences.

Chapter 5: The Healing Types

The Liberator is the kind of type that will help someone who's stuck in a situation of his or her own making. An example would be helping a friend study for a test because he can't understand the material and is failing the class. The specialty of the Liberator is helping people become unstuck or freeing them from feeling trapped.

The Advocate will speak up for those who don't have the capacity to speak up for themselves. Much of the work the Advocate will do is verbal and in defense of someone.

How can this type be a challenge?

The Rescuer can become too involved in the troubles of others and end up becoming the victim as well. More often, though, he is misunderstood and taken for a being nosy or, worse, a bully. Just because his intentions are pure doesn't mean others will see that. They may just see a loudmouth tough guy who can't mind his own business. If the Rescuer is a girl, she may end up suffering teasing and ridicule for being a goody-two-shoes because she's always standing up for people.

The Rescuer gets such a rush from helping people or rescuing animals he can't stop. He'll start to "attract" them because he's on the lookout for anyone who or anything that needs to be rescued. He may find lost animals as easy as most of us find our shoes. He'll come home talking about yet another person he stood up for. It may become consuming.

This can be very disconcerting for parents. It's not fun having to tell your tender-hearted Rescuer child that you just can't take in another animal. It would worry any parent to hear about the near-fights her son got into at school in an effort to help someone.

Okay, so now what do I do?

Find a shelter that takes good care of rescue animals. When

Family Types

he brings home another helpless animal, you'll know right where to go. Once a child zones in on animals that are in need, there will never be a shortage of possibilities. He'll be able to spot them anywhere, even on vacation. A parent of the Rescuer type needs a plan for where to bring the sad creatures before the house becomes overrun with them.

If your Rescuer is having trouble in school because he can't stand to see people bullied, and he's now being bullied, it's definitely time to meet with the teachers and principal. Teachers understand the differences in children, and explaining this insight could help protect the child from becoming perceived as a bully. Also, the Rescuer needs safe people to talk to when he sees someone in trouble. Try to teach your Rescuer that he needs other adults to help him help others. It's not entirely his responsibility.

Any Rescuer needs to unwind after an incident. It's a great time to listen without judgment and convey the wisdom that all Rescuers need to learn. These teachings include: Only help those who are asking for help. Ask teachers and those who are in higher authority to help those who need it. Don't escalate a situation out of pride. Only do the minimum needed to protect someone; don't take vengeance.

How to be with this type:

The child with the Rescuer type is courageous and tender-hearted. He's a reminder of the best in human nature. He may keep parents up at night worried that he will get into trouble unfairly, but with guidance and understanding he'll learn to make fewer mistakes and get into less trouble.

If he's decided to save the world, he'll need to learn that it's not his job alone. There are many, many Rescuers out there. It's not necessary to do more than what can be done well. When his efforts are in balance, he'll be able to help even more.

Companion/BFF

**She always has a best friend.
She's giving and loyal.**

Is this your child?

Since she was very little she's always had a best friend. The best friend may have changed over the years, but there has always been one special someone she has been closest to. Although she can play by herself, she's most content with one other person.

It may seem like only the most anti-social would not have this type, and nearly everyone with any friends is included. The child with the Companion type will not feel as comfortable playing with a group of friends as she will one-on-one. Also, her chosen BFF will be fairly consistent and not change from month to month. By 10 years old she may have had only two or three best friends, while others may have had many more.

This type is special in that she embodies a sweetness and tenderness that we all could only dream of in our relationships. She will model how the dearest of friendships function, with loyalty and generosity.

What brings out the best in this type?

Because the Companion type is so content when she is with that special person, she will be very happy during play dates. There will be little squabbling between the friends because they both put the friendship above other desires. If the child with the Companion has a friend who also has this type, the relationship will be sweet and easy to maintain.

What brings out the worst in this type?

A child with the Companion type may have a lot of stress and drama if she pairs herself with someone who is domineering. Because the Companion is so giving, she may find herself controlled and stifled by others who don't share her generosity. It can be heartbreaking for a parent to see their child struggling to stay happy in a friendship that takes too much work to please the other.

Sometimes a child with the Companion type has a hard time standing up for what she wants because she's afraid of upsetting and alienating her friend. She may not have developed the skills it takes to ask for what she wants without thinking she sounds selfish. Many girls grow into adults without this essential skill, but if she has the Companion type she may be more adversely affected than others. The ability to speak up for oneself is one of the most difficult yet most important issues to address if your child has this type.

Okay, so now what do I do?

If your child is struggling with a friendship that unfairly takes advantage of her commitment, she will likely want to talk with you about her troubles. As parents we are in an ideal position to help our Companion child develop her voice in a relationship. Listening to her complaints and offering advice and comfort are essential.

Perhaps the hardest thing for a parent to do is allow the friendship to exist for as long as it takes for the child to learn how to stand up for herself. We may want to tell our child that she needs to find a new friend and abandon this one, but

Chapter 5: The Healing Types

that would be the worst thing to do. Unless there is a situation in which your child is physically threatened or emotionally abused, it may be more effective to let the frustration build up and strengthen the child's own resolve to change things.

Often, as parents, we can tell that our children don't have the heart or capability to speak up for themselves, so we want to do it for them. We can't stand the unfair struggle that they are dealing with, and in trying to make things right and fair, we take away the chance for our children to learn how to do it for themselves. Allowing a child to stay in the unfair friendship, yet supporting and reminding her about what a good friend does, is a powerful combination that will eventually yield results.

The Companion will break an unfair friendship eventually, and with her own kind of resolve, when she's had enough. She must learn this skill as early as possible, or she may never believe she can speak up for herself, repeating the pattern again and again.

How to be with this type:

A child with the Companion type who has found a friend with mutual values is a very happy person. She will be content and peaceful. If she is in a challenging friendship, it is time for her to learn how to speak up for herself. It may be many months of struggle, but take comfort in knowing that when she finally stands up for herself she will have changed the next friendship for the better.

Once she knows she may lose a friend but eventually gain another, better friend, she will be destined to a lifetime of sweet companionship.

Guide / Mentor

He desires to help others so they can help themselves.

Is this your child?

He likes to tell people how to do something so they can do it by themselves. He's similar to a Teacher in that he wants to share knowledge and wisdom, but this type is different in that he only wants to see students learn so they can use it on their own. While a Teacher may like to share the same information again and again, the Guide likes to share knowledge as needed and then move on.

A child with the Guide type can give directions well, both for places but also how to get something done. He is a smart and thoughtful person, and he can easily assess how a task needs to be done. He can take a project and break it down into steps that someone can follow.

A Teacher is like a textbook and a Guide is like a workbook. A Teacher has the facts, and a Guide puts those facts to use.

What brings out the best in this type?

When someone is struggling with a problem, either a physical or emotional, the Guide is brilliant at walking him or her through the solution. He may go step-by-step, or give just enough information so the person can do the rest on his or her own. An example is helping someone with a project or craft.

Chapter 5: The Healing Types

A Guide will systematically show how it's done. Having a task with an obvious end result will bring out his talent.

A slightly different version of the Guide is the Mentor. The Mentor will do the task himself as an example for others to follow. Neither the Guide nor the Mentor is bossy or domineering unless the student refuses to follow the directions. Then the difficult side of this type may come out.

How can this type be a challenge?

Because the Guide has an amazing ability to see quickly how a project can turn out or a problem can be solved, it is hard to accept when others have a different view that he believes may not turn out so well. The Guide is incredibly smart and insightful, but this can make him very impatient with others. He may be happy at first to help someone, but the minute they want to go about it another way, he's sure the person is wrong.

As the parent, we may be able to tell him that it's wise to give the other person in the student role a chance and see how another path may turn out. This will be very difficult for the Guide. It's not that he wants to be in charge, but he really wants things to turn out "right." Parents may find themselves telling their Guide that it doesn't have to be perfect. That phrase, "it doesn't have to be perfect," is a sure sign that the Guide has decided on the path or method, and is now completely set on it. This rigid temperament can be difficult for anyone watching or receiving the help.

Okay, so now what do I do?

If a parent has noticed that her child with the Guide type becomes frustrated and pushy if things don't go his way, it's time to take a look at how the child is rewarded for his efforts. It may seem counter-intuitive to address the time when things

Family Types

go well and the Guide has helped someone, but this is the kind of situation that feeds his rigid nature.

When a child with the Guide type helps someone and the student is receptive, it's a match made in heaven, and the Guide will experience very strong positive feelings. That's also when we pat him on the back for what he did and the feelings get even stronger. While this may seem like only a good thing, it reinforces a time when the student was completely willing to listen to the Guide.

But in life, students often don't want to listen to everything someone has to teach. People want to feel success based on their own merits, so frequently the Guide will have to work with a half-listening student.

Further, people often have ideas of their own that they want to test, and once the Guide has gotten them unstuck, they may want take off on their own in a new direction.

The Guide needs to learn that there is great reward in helping others only as far as they are willing to go. If he puts too much attention on the end result or the finished product, he'll lose sight of the people he is helping.

As parents, it's best to focus our encouragement on how our child with the Guide type treated the student. We can tell our child that we are proud of how he honored and respected the needs and desires of the student, and pay less attention to the accomplished task instead. If the Guide learns to feel satisfaction from how well he treated someone, it will become more important than the goal itself. Then with every engagement he's sure to find contentment.

How to be with this type:

Taking care to reinforce the cooperative nature of your child is an important step in his healthy development. It's common to put our focus on the outcome of a project or solution, but it will only reinforce that aspect. The best kind of guidance and mentoring includes allowing the student to continue or complete the task on his or her own so the student can experience the pleasure of success. When a child with the Guide type learns that the success of others is also his own, he can find more fulfillment and ease in the process of getting there, and not just at the end.

Chapter 6
The Creative Types

Artist

Scribe/Historian

Pioneer

Networker/Gossip

Engineer

Athlete/Winner

Dilettante

Nearly every child will have one of these types. It's the part of each of us that must "do something," and the types in this category show us how we do what we do. These are not as much about solving problems or relating to other people, but rather how your child sees the world and takes it in.

The Artist gives us a visual or audible reflection of what the world is like in their eyes. The Scribe/Historian appreciates and cherishes history and all things from the past. The Pioneer wants to experience the world outside of his usual boundaries. The Networker/Gossip studies how people come together to be more than the sum of the parts. The Engineer breaks the old habits of problem-solving, and ventures into uncomfortable yet new, possible realms.

The Athlete/Winner pushes the limitations of the human body to do what we haven't yet seen. The Dilettante is able to try new things and quickly find proficiency, where others may struggle to even begin.

Each of these types can be either a boy or a girl. They each help us see the possibilities that the world can offer us.

Artist

**She loves to perform, sing, or create.
She needs to share what she creates with others.**

Is this your child?

She can spend hours drawing, painting, or creating. She may create with paper or toys, or any kind of material. She may create things that are a beautiful version of what she sees, or maybe a symbolic version that is different from what others would see.

An Artist takes a certain aspect or element of life and re-creates it in another way.

If she's a performer, she may love to act or sing. Children who hear a beautiful song and try to sing it are trying to experience the song more fully. Children who act out a scene that's entertaining or dress up like someone else are reproducing something special about human nature.

If a child writes stories or music, it is because she sees it or hears it in her mind, and wants others to experience it. The Artist rarely keeps her art to herself.

What brings out the best in this type?

The best environment for children to create in includes free time, basic supplies, and no judgment from others.

Free time to play and explore will stoke the creative fires. When a creative child has too much structure or responsibility,

Chapter 6: The Creative Types

she'll begin to feel stifled and restless. Free time does not include watching TV or playing with electronics. TV or video games are a distraction, and they burn the energy that could be used to create. An Artist must have time set aside regularly when the TV and video games are off.

If art supplies or musical instruments are available, a child with the Artist type will be drawn to use them. The more she can play with and use these things without anyone telling her what to do or how to do it, the more she'll feel free to create. When she feels free, the most astonishing and amazing things come forth.

Although music or art lessons help develop skills for the Artist, lessons should be a complement to what the child enjoys. When the Artist feels too much pressure to do something the "right" way, natural creativity can become stifled.

What can be a challenge with this type?

One area of difficulty is that the Artist can take herself too seriously, and demand more and more from her family. Whether it's quiet space to work, supplies, or attention from her parents, she may need so much that the rest of the family ends up with less than they need. Siblings may grow resentful of the time and energy spent on the one child. The Artist may insist that in order to "do her art" everyone must leave her in peace. The performer may insist that her family watch every creative interlude. The child with the Artist type can be demanding.

The Artist may begin to feel that she can't produce unless the environment is perfect. She may get to the point where she can't feel satisfied or accomplished. She may grow moody without her special art space, almost addicted to needing it.

An Artist may demand that no one judge her negatively. She may become thin skinned and oversensitive to any critiquing.

Family Types

Yet at the same time she may be very critical of others who create. The more serious she takes herself, the more critical she'll be of others.

Okay, so now what do I do?

Balance is not easy for the child with the Artist type. She will likely struggle with it her whole life. That may be a blessing in disguise if she can learn some essential techniques early in life. When anyone struggles with balance, the "cure is in the disease." The struggle itself is the way to bring in balance.

Most people are not born with discipline and will have to develop it. The best motivation to learn discipline is when things around us are distracting, but we have to focus anyway. When the Artist becomes demanding and *must* create, a parent can attach a reward of "creating time" in exchange for self-discipline.

For example, time and freedom to create can be given after the child has picked up her room and read a short book to a sibling. Another example is withholding creative time if the child's negative attitude is affecting others. Allowing the child to create trouble so she can go do what she wants, even if it's a healthy, creative endeavor, is a recipe for family discord. Artist types notoriously have this issue.

If parents take the need to create seriously, and reinforce the immense value it is to the child by using creative time as a reward for kind and patient behavior, the attitude of demanding and insisting will be lessened. No matter how amazing the child is, it cannot be at a cost to the family members' relationship. Creating is very fulfilling, but it doesn't trump a family life of kindness and respect.

Another element of the Artist that can be difficult is her sensitivity about her work. Thin-skinned and oversensitive, she may grow to demand only positive feedback from others, especially her parents. If a parent is lucky enough to recognize this early, she may be able to exercise honesty about her child's work. While there are times when it is not necessary to tell your child you don't like the work, it is always a bad idea to fib and say you do in order to spare her feelings.

One method of helping the Artist gain the ability to hear a critique of her work is to ask her to do it herself. If she wants to know your opinion, ask her to tell you hers first. The hardest time to have the Artist type as a child is when she thinks: "What will others think of it?" It's important for her to develop her own critiquing skills early. It's an important job for a parent to help her listen to her own voice. Often, the Artist is most critical when she's thinking for others; her own true voice is usually pleased, at least to a degree. Help the Artist find perspective in her own words.

How to be with this type:

The Artist is an exciting and fun type. She will bring fresh, new ideas to families, and likely strive for very high standards. The Artist is a sort of visionary, and that comes with intense feelings. Although it is ideal to have space and materials for her to create, any Artist will eventually have to work within confines. Not all creative careers come with plenty of time and money. If she can learn to work with what is available, it will give her the strength to work in any circumstances.

Because her art can be the most important thing to her, it is imperative she learn that her treatment of other people must be a priority. Respect for others will create self-respect and a more fulfilling career. Very few people end up in happy solitary lives. Healthy relationships are paramount, and the fulfillment of art must not trample them.

Although the Artist will need to learn how to accept criticism, the priority is teaching her to listen to her own

Family Types

opinions, and sometimes even ignoring others'. When she can give herself an honest and balanced assessment, she'll be able to keep others' opinions in perspective. This will go a long way to temper her critical nature as well.

It can be exciting to see the work that children produce. So many Artist types show their genius early in life. While no amount of talent can foretell an easy road to success, when an Artist is able to relate to her family well and joyfully create when she can, she will be well on her way to a fulfilling life.

Scribe/Historian

**He sees value in things that are old.
He appreciates history and how it is still useful today.**

Is this your child?

He loves his old toys and has a hard time parting with them. He can be sentimental, especially with his oldest things. He likes to learn about history and may have a particular interest in one era. He may like people who are much older than him more than other children would. He enjoys stories that people tell from when they were young.

What brings out the best in this type?

Learning about his interest will always light him up. If he likes old cars, he'll love to go to a classic car show. If he loves old music, he may enjoy listening to someone's old record collection. Books and TV shows about his interest will always keep him occupied. He may enjoy starting a collection of some sort around his favorite subject. If a family trip includes his favorite interest, like a trip to a museum, he will never forget it.

How can this type be a challenge?

Sometimes the Scribe gets so enamored of his interest he is blind to anything else. For example, if he likes old cars he may learn so much about them that he will develop a belief that nothing new is as good as the old. For an old music aficionado, all new music is subpar.

The child with the Scribe type can become locked in his opinion and refuse to consider any other view. Even when evidence of the value of the new item is available, the Scribe may insist it's not relevant.

The Scribe loves to collect things about his favorite subject, and sometimes his collection of old things is so big he can't make room for anything new. He can lose the perspective about what is truly a quality item and what is just old. To him "old" means "quality," even if it obviously is not. He may be unwilling to give up junk and end up with too much valueless stuff.

Okay, so now what do I do?

Parents may think that giving the child new items will push out the old ones. That isn't often the case with the Scribe. The more a child with the Scribe type is pushed to give up the old, the more he'll push back. The Scribe can be a very obstinate type, refusing all reason. He'll have to be given boundaries and made to edit his own collection.

For example, a Scribe has an awesome model airplane collection that has gotten out of control. Obviously some of the planes are a wreck and need to be trashed. A parent may suggest this, but the child is adamantly against it. The tug-o-war begins.

It is better to tell the Scribe that his amazing collection must be trimmed to fit a certain space. He can keep anything that fits within that space. The rest will have to find a new home. It's likely the idea of throwing anything away will upset him, so a donation to an organization like the Salvation Army may be better accepted. If he can surrender some of his collection, particularly the ones he doesn't enjoy, the rest will be more

Chapter 6: The Creative Types

beautiful and enjoyable. He'll learn that having the best of the best is wonderful.

It's hard to watch a Scribe miss out on some of the new things that people have, but as understanding parents we have to accept that what truly brings him joy is the old. He really likes it better. The more we accept this, the more willing he will be to try out new things.

How to be with this type:

Avoiding the tug-o-war is important to getting along with the Scribe. Setting early boundaries and giving him the chance to decide how to live within those boundaries will help him in the future. The collections of Scribes can overrun a house if left unchecked.

Because the Scribe believes he's preserving history, he may forget that he lives now. Giving him a variety of fun things to learn about will help him keep his passion in perspective. Coupled with the understanding that he prefers old things to new, parents can keep balance at home.

Pioneer

She has to do things in a way that no one has done before.

Is this your child?

The child with the Pioneer type seems to always take the road less traveled. If a task is often done one way, she'll try another way. She gets bored easily when something has to be repeated. She'll change her routines often, from where she does her homework to where she eats her meals. She loves the thrill of trying something new. If she's going to a new restaurant she may try things on the menu that are unusual.

What brings out the best in this type?

The child with the Pioneer type is a lot of fun, because she's willing to try anything. She'll try new foods, projects, and games, and make new friends easily. She'll change her morning routine and ask to go to school a different way. She doesn't like to stay home too much and will be happy just going for a drive to see the sights, as long as the route is new. She is an easy child to take on vacation as long as there isn't too much sitting around and relaxing.

How can this type be a challenge?

She'll get bored easily and can become unpredictable to locate if she's allowed to roam. It can become frustrating to a

Chapter 6: The Creative Types

parent who is constantly looking for her child and wondering at which neighbor's house she is now—and if she's not allowed to roam, it can be exhausting to a parent to keep her entertained.

Although she'll enjoy trying new activities, she'll even try to make those happen in a way that no one has tried. For example, if she gets a new game, she'll want to try it with different rules. Not all other children will appreciate, or even like it.

Okay, so now what do I do?

The child with the Pioneer type is exciting and will push others outside their comfort zone. If a parent can recognize that it is often fun to do new things, although inconvenient at times, it will help to calm the worries that go with change. It will be important to teach the child with the Pioneer type that there are times to relax and enjoy themselves where they are.

Making time to explore and try new things with the Pioneer will help her feel validated and close to her parents and family members. It would be unfortunate for the Pioneer to end up lonely because no one will accompany her on adventure. With regular doses of new and exciting things, the Pioneer can learn to make time to settle down and be with her family in a structured and planned environment.

An example would be having family movie night every Friday but then Saturday will be the day to go to a festival or museum or someplace new. Ideally the child with the Pioneer type would have a neighborhood of friends to visit, but in the least a parent could make play dates for the child so she will have the change she craves.

How to be with this type:

It may seem that the child with the Pioneer type is high-maintenance, and when she's young she may be. If she's unable to feed her spirit for the new, she may make trouble at home just for the rush of excitement. It's worth recognizing her need and nourishing it as much as possible. Once she's had her fresh experiences, she should able to relax easier into the routine of home life.

In the very least, parents can be assured that their Pioneer will grow into independence easily and take off as soon as she's ready. She'll find fun and excitement wherever she goes, and will surely have some great stories to tell when she returns.

Networker/Gossip

**She loves to share information that is helpful.
She can bring people together for the good of everyone.**

Is this your child?

She loves to talk. She loves to ask personal questions and gives you her complete focus. She's curious and a great listener. She has strong opinions and is fearless to say them.

She knows everything that's going on with everyone. She likes to hear about the good, the bad, and everything in between. Her ability to retain personal details about people is impressive. Her memory is exceptional, particularly about what people do or say.

What brings out the best in this type?

Social activities are always fun for a Networker. Her insatiable interest in people is the driving force for her to get out and visit. She'll have many friends, in many different circles. Her favorite activities will be listening and telling stories about others.

The life's purpose of a child with the Networker or Gossip type is to bring people together. Helping people make connections that create collaboration is an essential skill for the betterment of the planet. Parents should be proud that their child has a destiny to help people connect. Often parents just think that they have a social butterfly, and that's all there is to

Family Types

it, but a child that can talk to anyone, remember details about them, and share information about others, can do many great things with her life.

How is this type a challenge?

She can't keep secrets very well. She can be inappropriate about what she tells people, sharing information that's private. She's not embarrassed by what she talks about and even enjoys sharing information that is salacious. She gets a rush when she figures out a secret and can be very persistent if she knows you're keeping one. She'll say out loud, in front of others, that you're incorrect if she thinks you're changing the facts. This can be very embarrassing.

Okay, so now what do I do?

A child with the Gossip type wants to know the truth, and will blurt out the truth as she sees fit. Sometimes she doesn't realize that certain information is no one's business. She'll have a habit of speaking too much about others her whole life, but don't give up teaching her about when it's unacceptable. Although a parent shouldn't humiliate her in front of others in order to teach her to stop, it's still important to do whatever it takes to get her to stop.

Certainly, though, the most powerful response to a Gossip who is being insensitive about other people is using kindness as an example. Learning the value of kindness is a key to helping the Gossip see what is acceptable and what is not. If there can be a theme that goes hand in hand with helping this type become a positive influence instead of negative, it is kindness.

Sometimes the Gossip can be taught to think before she says something, but this type really doesn't know what to think, unless she's actually taught what kindness means. Making a concerted effort to define kindness so she completely

Chapter 6: The Creative Types

understands is imperative. She just won't pick up on the meaning as easily as most others. It may be impossible to stop her in the moment if she's spoken unkindly of others, but if she can be taken aside and not embarrassed herself, she may be more receptive to her parents' guidance.

Additionally, a Gossip needs to learn how to apologize. A child with the Gossip type will always struggle with saying things that hurt others. She'll do it throughout her youth even with the best parenting. Not all of it can be stopped, so learning how to say she's sorry will help her recover relationships and her own self-worth. She needs to know that sometimes people will stop trusting her even after she says she's sorry, and that's part of what she will have to handle. Even a young child can learn that making amends is essential if someone is hurt by what she said. She'll need to learn that an apology can go far to mend hurt feelings and it's worth saying.

How to be with this type:

If being nosy or blurting out private information is her weakness, a child with the Gossip type can learn to speak in a way that won't hurt others. It takes a very patient and kind parent to manage the vivaciousness of the Gossip. Treating her with kindness and helping her learn the value of kindness will give her the power to use her talent for good. Once she learns the importance of bringing people together, and that her purpose in life is to do that, she'll be a gift to all her friends and family.

From sales, politics, and mediating, to networking and socializing, the Networker and Gossip types are modern-day essentials. Because many people struggle to connect with others, she'll be the bridge that can bring them together.

Engineer

He's a problem-solver.
He is down to earth and practical.

Is this your child?

He loves to see how things work. He'll take things apart then put them back together. He loves creative construction toys. If there is problem to be solved, he'll come up with an answer. He'll try to figure out the quickest way to get something done.

What can bring out the best in this type?

Allowing a child with the Engineer type to help solve problems will create self-confidence. Even at a young age, asking his opinion about something will enliven him and validate his passion for solutions. He's always thinking about how things work and how to make things better, so any time his ideas are requested, he is learning how to apply his passion.

The Engineer type is easy to spot because he usually will speak up if he thinks he can help. This type is vivacious and rarely shy. Even the youngest of children have ideas about how to do things, and if he is an Engineer you may be pleasantly surprised by his bright ideas.

How can this type be a challenge?

Even though he is eager to help solve problems, many of his ideas don't take other people's needs into consideration. He may

Chapter 6: The Creative Types

even sound a little bossy at times when he's sure he knows the best method. The hardest part about living with the Engineer type is when he finds a solution that is very inconvenient to accomplish. Even when a parent tries to explain this, he's sure he's right and the inconvenience issue doesn't matter.

Because he can envision a solution very clearly in his mind, but he lacks the empathy for the people involved, it can be hard to convince him his idea is flawed. Most children develop empathy and the ability to consider the feelings of others eventually, but for an Engineer type this will be his greatest weakness.

For example, a child with the Engineer type suggests the best way to play a game so that several children get a turn. The problem, though, is that more children want to play than his organized method allows. He can get so caught up in his "best" method that he won't be able to work with everyone. He may become frustrated when the rules must be changed to accommodate everyone.

Okay, so now what do I do?

The more times the Engineer can return to his original solution and revamp it to accommodate people, the better he will be at anything he chooses to do as an adult. If a parent can tell her child that his solution is good but needs to still be better, and then allow him to rework the problem, he will likely learn to be more flexible. Once he learns flexibility, he can approach many more problems with useful solutions. It would be a disservice to the Engineer to throw out his entire idea without letting him try to rework it first.

Too many young children are full of ideas that adults disregard because the children's thoughts sound difficult or inconvenient. Sadly, many children with the Engineer type grow up never learning the skills it takes to really make an

Family Types

impact on people. Sometimes these children become adults who have a hard time collaborating with coworkers. They even end up isolated and marginalized simply because they haven't realized that their solutions need a second look and some reorganizing.

How to be with this type:

The best part about the Engineer is that he is often willing to help—that is, as long as his ideas are considered. It is important for these children to have experiences where adults listen and implement what they envision. Nothing can be more validating and rewarding for children with this type.

Using all of his ideas, no matter how inconvenient, can spoil the Engineer and stunt his ability to consider the impact of his wishes. In order to grow into a balanced adult, he must learn the art of working with others and within the nature of people. If he's given tasks that press him to think of what people want, not just a perfect solution regardless of people, he'll be better equipped as an adult.

Athlete/Winner

She has the ability to push herself beyond her comfort zone in order to succeed.

Is this your child?

She's competitive and simply has to win. She will get very upset if she doesn't win and can seem spoiled. She has a high pain tolerance and won't give up the way most others will. She'll love to play games and sports that are challenging.

What brings out the best in this type?

If she can play it and win it, she'll like it. It may be a classic board game or competitive sports, but no matter the venue, she'll give it her all. If a task can be turned into a competitive challenge, she'll like it more. It's not enough to race against the clock; she'll want a challenger to face off with.

She'll likely learn self-discipline easily, especially if she's given a standard to meet. If her grades are measured with a specific minimum requirement, she'll try to meet it. It's even better for her if she can compete with a sibling.

How can this type be a challenge?

Competitiveness between siblings is already common, but if one sibling has an Athlete type it will be much worse. Any child with this type will try to seek out a challenger, and the most convenient ones are her siblings. If she's playing a game

Family Types

and it appears she's about to lose, it can seem like World War II broke out. Other children will be confused because the Athlete becomes so upset over a board game.

It can be embarrassing for parents if their child breaks down into tears at a loss on the playground. Often parents are to blame when a child becomes hysterical because she didn't win. Any parent who has had their child embarrass them can attest that they did not create the emotion overload in their child, but may lack the skills to avoid it. Sometimes parents take their Athlete children out of competitive activities because it is too difficult to stop the meltdowns.

Another area of concern for the child with the Athlete type is that she may cheat at games in order to win them. It's not uncommon for children to do this, but the Athlete has a propensity to bend the rules more than others. Most parents will recognize this issue and deal with it accordingly. Obviously it should not be tolerated at all. Even though parents can sense how upsetting it is for their child to lose, it will not damage her self-esteem to experience it. A true Athlete will always come back and try again.

Okay, so now what do I do?

To the child with the Athlete type, winning is everything. It's not that she wants to win: She needs to win. Once parents can understand that the Athlete will always have this intense desire and that it cannot be squelched, we can then turn our attention to channeling it. From the time the Athlete is very young, it's better to give her comfort when she loses than a scolding for unsportsmanlike conduct. She will be slow to develop grace, but it will happen. It will happen quicker if she's given compassion.

Just dealing with hysterics isn't enough. After the game is over and the hysterics have passed, it's important for parents

Chapter 6: The Creative Types

to talk with their child about how to behave after a loss. Recommending that the child try to wait until getting home to fuss can be an eventual goal. As long as the child feels compassion and that she will be heard at some point, she will likely learn to hold on to her feelings until a better time.

Children who are simply scolded and refused empathy often grow more determined to express how upset they are, and the problem may persist. Parents may dread starting new activities because they know she'll end up so upset. It's not spoiling her to give her a hug and a listening ear. Once she's finally done crying, she will likely go back for another try. Eventually she'll find an appropriate way to express her disappointment, although it will always be intense.

How to be with this type:

Most of our Olympians have this type. It takes so much perseverance and strength to become the best of the best. Any child with this type will find success at something. They just won't give up. Even though their feelings of disappointment are intense, those are the same feelings that will keep them pushing their limits long after others have quit.

Allowing the competitive nature of the Athlete type to have its expression is very important to healthy growth. An Athlete needs a challenge. Refusing to allow cheating, even if it seems easier, will help her learn the true satisfaction of a fair win. And helping her channel her loss into a desire to get back out and try will help her truly become the best at whatever she chooses to do.

Dilettante

She loves to try new creative things but has a hard time sticking with it until she's proficient.

Is this your child?

She's ready and willing to try the next exciting thing. It may be a new musical instrument, dance class, or a new video game. She's sure it will be so fun and that she'll want to keep doing it, but she loses interest quickly. She may want to try a new sport, but midway through each season she'll get bored and ask to quit altogether.

What brings out the best in this type?

The child with the Dilettante type is fearless at trying new things. Her thirst for new and exciting activities is endless. She may be very good at them initially, showing talent and potential, but as soon as practice becomes mundane she'll lose interest. Usually a Dilettante is full of talent and begins each new interest with lots of energy. The start of every new activity is her favorite time.

How can this type be a challenge?

Her giving up on every new activity after a few months can be frustrating to any parent. Usually there is financial investment and time spent attending practices or lessons. This

Chapter 6: The Creative Types

can feel like such a waste. Parents eventually resist trying new things with their child because the pattern is so predictable.

Okay, so now what do I do?

What's worse: wasting time and money on an activity that will not be pursued, or wasting the potential talent in your child? This is not meant to be a joke. Parents can really struggle to decide what's important. It can be especially challenging if we are trying to give our little ones the chances we didn't have.

By the time parents have experienced this pattern, the child with the Dilettante type is old enough to have some goals set up. Before committing to the new endeavor, it is important to decide how long she must stick with it—without complaint—before having the option to quit.

With sports it may be that she has to finish out the season. With music or dance lessons it may be that she has to continue until the recital is over. It's always good to give her a tangible and exact finish line that she can understand. For some children it may even help to give her a calendar for her room with the appropriate dates marked down.

Once the child is clear about what the commitment is, and is limited to only that endeavor, she will have a better chance of finishing the season or year. Although she may try something else after that, at least she's learning that commitment takes endurance.

How to be with this type:

Often children simply lack the understanding that the lessons have a purpose more than just learning. A marker or indicator to show how far she's come, coupled with a reward of celebration at the end, can help her learn the purpose of trying something new. Each new skill she learns is hers to keep and use for the rest of her life. That is cause for celebration.

One of the hardest issues with the Dilettante is when she starts to complain that she is tired of the lessons. This can really wear down a parent. It's one of the most grueling aspects of parenting. It may be worth refusing to begin the next exciting thing because the child complained so much. Refusing to start something new in response to too much complaining can really help the Dilettante realize the value of an opportunity. The more she feels like she missed out, the more determined she'll be to stick it out the next time.

And parents shouldn't worry that their multi-talented child missed out because they had to say "No more." A new and exciting opportunity is just around the corner, and it won't be long before your Dilettante will want to try another activity.

Chapter 7
The Action Types

Hero/Heroine

Coward/Bully

Gambler/Risk-Taker

Rebel/Revolutionary

Detective/Spy

Midas/Miser

The types that fit the Action category are two sides of the same coin. Each type here is notorious for one aspect of the personality, but each has an inverse opposite that goes hand-in-hand. Often we see just the negative aspect of these, as in the Gambler, but once we understand the deeper meaning and purpose of each type, the flip side is apparent and has the potential to be positive.

Each can be either male or female, and although I designate a gender, it is only for ease of reading. Please feel free to interpret the gender differently.

Children who have one of the Action types can be difficult to live with because they tend to rock the boat. They are full of energy, and can be unpredictable or surprising in their behaviors. These children keep their parents on their toes and test the patience of everyone. It takes a very wise and compassionate person to see through the dynamic behavior and avoid getting flustered.

If you tend to find yourself sometimes shocked and surprised by your child, take a close look at these types and the types in the next category – (the Wild Card types). If you're lucky enough to have a child with one of these types, you may feel sometimes that it's a curse. Although your family life tends to be less than peaceful, it's a sure sign that change is happening.

Just like a storm that blows through, the Action and Wild Card types leave in their wake a fresh new start. If it weren't for the rain, new flowers could not grow.

Hero/Heroine

In order to accomplish what he wants, he must go alone.

Is this your child?

He loves to take on goals and is happy to do it by himself. He's not interested in team activities unless he is the key to success, like the quarterback of the football team. He can be independent or even a little anti-social, but it's usually only when he's trying to accomplish something. He has a fearless way of doing things that can make parents nervous, but the child with the Hero type doesn't see danger as something to avoid.

What brings out the best in this type?

We often associate the Hero type with accomplishment of a physical goal, as in sports. Children who are drawn to join the armed forces so they can do something challenging and exciting have this type. Girls who put friendships on hold in order to do something new and exciting have the Heroine type. The children who have this type shake up the relationship dynamics expected of them and endeavor to do something never done before.

For example, if all the boys in a family go to the same school, the Hero may decide to go to another school. He or she won't do it because of rebellion, but because it's a new and difficult challenge.

Chapter 7: The Action Types

How can this type be a challenge?

Because these children leave the safety and comfort of family and friends, it can make parents feel worried or even rejected. If the family unit depends on each other for support, but the child with the Hero does not, it can shake the system. Often, the challenge of having a child with the Hero type is feeling as though he doesn't need the family. This disconnect can be difficult for parents who want to share in their child's life and experiences.

Although this may seem like a rebellion, the child with the Hero type is not acting out of frustration or anger, but acting on inspiration and desire. Only when parents and friends start pressuring the Hero to stay within his circle does the struggle begin—and it inevitably will happen.

The child with the Hero type is merely moving toward a goal, or desire for something more. Along the way, he leaves behind something that was important to his family's culture. This disturbs the system, and the family members pressure him into returning to the way things were. An example may be an adolescent who wants to try a new church or join a group for missionary work.

Okay, so now what do I do?

Once a parent accepts that there will always be unconventional things their child asks or tries to do, then it's a matter of finding a comfortable middle. The more a parent squashes the ideas of the child, the stronger the desire will be. Obviously letting a child follow all of his whims, regardless of safety and well-being, is not wise, but making a concerted effort to do something that will satisfy the urge will help.

Let's say a teen with the Hero type wants to travel to another country as an exchange student. This is a new and unusual idea for the family. It may also be too expensive. But because the Hero will likely do anything to accomplish this goal, even over the long term, it may be something worth trying to plan. To the Hero, even if it takes years of excellent grades, scholarships, and saving up, he will be willing to do it all. Once the child with the Hero type decides on a goal, no matter how long it takes, he'll make it happen.

Sometimes parents can tell that the goal is not only lofty, but that the inspiration comes from a silly place. Maybe the child who wants to travel really just wants to get away from his siblings for a while. If the child truly has a Hero type within him, it doesn't matter the root of the desire. The longer it takes to get there, the more sincere and passionate the Hero becomes. He'll find other reasons, and they'll be better than the first.

How to be with this type:

If parents can take the time to discuss and plan a possible path toward the goal, the Hero will learn to do the same as he matures. If the plan has to be revisited and revised, that is an important skill this type will need in life. The only path that will surely bring strife and worry is if the parents simply refuse to entertain their child's unusual requests. Nothing will be more devastating and heartbreaking to the child. Not all journeys of the Hero type can happen while he's a child, but if parents can appreciate the bravery and drive of their child, it will do much to help the Hero once he is on his own.

Bully/Coward

She uses physical or mental strength to protect herself from getting hurt.

Is this your child?

No one will admit his or her child has this type, especially in today's "no tolerance" world, but this is a very common type and worth understanding. Most children will bully another sometime in their life. Some children do it a lot. The child with the Bully type will have a tendency to find weaker, perhaps smaller, more vulnerable children, and do or say things that hurt them. If a parent knows his or her child does this, it's likely that parent realizes that the child is acting out of feeling pain and fear. Nearly all children who have this type have experiences of being physically or emotionally abused at some point. The abuse could even have been from another Bully.

The child who's getting picked on doesn't realize the Bully is feeling pain or fear, though. In fact, it looks like the Bully is fine and happy. There is not one instance that a Bully strikes, physically or verbally, that is not filled with fear of pain.

What brings out the best in this type?

Obviously we think that a happy, safe environment would cure the Bully of her nature, or that if our child is raised in a kind and loving home she would not develop it. A Bully is not simply made by her environment. Instead, this child was born with a Bully tendency, and environment has played it up. All of us will experience having our boundaries crossed; there is no perfect childhood. We each learn to protect ourselves in our own way.

The Bully is simply protecting herself this way, and that will happen no matter what her upbringing. In the best environment, fear and pain may have been minimal—but still unavoidable. No matter the cause, if the behavior is part of the child's nature, things can be done to shape it into a more positive expression.

No one is lucky enough to grow up with zero difficulty, and the most powerful life skills often come out of overcoming challenges. Life's challenges are here like a weight-bearing exercise: They will help us grow stronger in the long run. Even someone with a Bully type has the potential for turning a vice into a gift.

If parents are trying to create a perfect home life in order to calm the Bully, they may be spinning their wheels. The way to help a child with this type is to teach skills that can be applied from within her. The purpose of this type is to develop bravery and self-worth. The only way to the other side is through using the type, not squelching or avoiding it.

How can this type be a challenge?

Any time our children do things that hurt others we will feel embarrassed and ashamed. No parents want to hear that their child is less than kind and gentle, but taking steps to stop the Bullying nature must be done with the utmost care so as not to feed it further. It can take all the energy and patience a parent can muster to maintain self-control when dealing with a child with the Bully type. It's not unusual to feel indignant and exasperated that the child is behaving this way. Often parents have been dealing with the issue for some time. It is a

Chapter 7: The Action Types

huge challenge to stay cool when our child acts well below our expectations. But stay cool we must.

Okay, so now what do I do?

Any time we get upset, and our child with the Bully type sees us ruffled, it will send a huge fear signal through their body. There is no way they will be able to hear one reprimand or piece of advice from us during those moments. They're just too scared to absorb the fact that they have to take responsibility. Taking responsibility and developing courage to do the right thing cannot grow as long as the child is afraid.

The first and most important tactic is to find a time when the child is not feeling or acting out of fear or anger. At that time, bring up the most recent incident in which the child was a Bully. Ask her to tell her side of the story. Usually she can give a reason for feeling upset or she can admit she wasn't acting her best.

This is the best time to issue a firm consequence for the behavior. The parent must remain calm, even a little upbeat, no matter what the child does. The consequence must also be firm. It must matter to the child.

For example, say your child calls another child a nasty, mean name. You hear about it later that day. Leave it alone until your child is in a calm and peaceful state, perhaps watching TV. Then ask your child what happened and why. First, acknowledge her response without judgment. Once the child knows she's heard, she will be able to listen. Tell her the rule of no bullying and that she broke the rule. Suggest a better response that would have avoided hurting the other person. Ask her if she could come up with a better response. Issue a consequence that can be put into place as soon as possible—no fussing, no anger, just calm but firm consequences.

Without adding to the drama, the Bully can only see her

Family Types

actions and the consequences of them. Nothing is feeding her fear and giving her a self-protection reaction. If enough of these interludes are strung together, the Bully will learn that she has other options and her reflex response is unrewarding.

How to be with this type:

Bullies try to avoid their feelings of fear and the pain of embarrassment by hurting others before they get hurt. Then they find themselves in more fear once their actions are found out, because parents and teachers are so upset. If parents can create an environment that deals with the behavior without feeding the root of it, it will help the child develop the capacity to use self-control.

With more feelings of safety, the child can learn self-control. With more self-control, the child can make better decisions simply because she's not feeling under fire inside. If the child continues to experience fearful situations, very little can be done to calm this nature.

If parents and teachers could see that the Bully has an over-stimulated fear response, it would be easier to avoid worsening it. It never means just letting the bullying happen. If consequences can be given in a calm and compassionate manner, it would help the Bully feel safe but accountable.

Only when a child feels safe can she begin to grow into a compassionate, courageous person.

Gambler/Risk-Taker

**He will try anything without thinking first.
He's fearless when it comes to taking risk.**

Is this your child?

He's a natural at doing tricks with his bike or skateboard. He'll try daredevil feats that elicit the awe of others. He's physical and rarely seen just sitting around. He'll leave the beaten path and explore where most kids would fear snakes and bugs. He will be unpredictable all his life and keep his parents worried often.

What brings out the best in this type?

He loves a challenge, like rock climbing or water skiing. If he isn't sure which path to take, he'll just follow his gut and go. Usually he picks a good one, or at least an interesting and exciting one. He loves to try new things and go new places. Like the Pioneer, he has a zest for adventure. For the Gambler that's not enough; there must also be some form of risk. He loves to overcome his fears, if he slows down long enough to feel them.

Some children with the Gambler type seem to have extra protection that keeps them from too much injury. Is it luck, angels, or a strong intuition that saves the Gambler from a bad situation? Parents may be frequently relieved and surprised their Gambler child escaped an injury yet again.

Family Types

Gamblers don't get lost easily, either. They have such a strong sense of guidance and intuition that they just seem to always know where they are.

How can this type be a challenge?

A child who loves to take great risks will bring worry and concern to his parents. He may annoy his teachers if he can't sit still for long. Because he may be an adrenalin junkie, school may be a challenge. He may get great grades, but his need for motion and stimulation may distract the others in class.

He may make his parents frustrated because he won't follow too many rules or respect boundaries. He's not trying to break them, but he is trying to see what would happen if he doesn't follow them. To the Gambler, this is exciting and fun. To his parents, it's exasperating.

Okay, so now what do I do?

The more the Gambler is given rules, the more he'll explore what will happen when he doesn't follow them. The fewer the rules between parents and the child with the Gambler type, the easier they are to uphold.

The Gambler doesn't think things through very much. He depends on his intuition. But without thinking he may find himself in trouble even after he's been warned. It's easier for the Gambler to learn something by physically experiencing it instead of just being told.

For example, the Gambler can be told: "Don't touch that, it's hot." He touches it anyway. He's learned. Often he has to learn the hard way. Very sweet and compassionate parents may feel they were not careful enough to explain the cost of touching something hot. In fact they may try to explain even more next time.

Whenever possible, giving the Gambler something physical

to teach with will help tremendously, like warming a cup of water until it's uncomfortable to the touch, but not burning. Have the child touch it and explain that that's "tiny hot," compared with "big hot" of the stove. With a physical experience, the Gambler will be able to hear the lesson better.

How to be with this type:

The child with the Gambler type needs a place to explore, but that still won't be enough. If parents can schedule activities that he finds exciting, it's well worth the effort.

Listen to his intuition; he's often correct. If he can slow down long enough to practice hearing his intuition, he will be better equipped to keep himself safe.

Rebel/Revolutionary

She will ignore established modes or systems and do things in a different way.

Is this your child?

If you say "up," she says "down." If you say "stop," she says "go." This child won't do what she's told. Or if she does, she'll undo it later. She doesn't want to work with others. She wants to do anything that the others aren't doing.

Parents of a child with the Rebel type have a challenge to deal with if they like things to follow tradition. The more parents enforce a structure or system, the more this child avoids or refuses to follow it.

What brings out the best in this type?

Historically, old and outdated systems have been torn down by the Rebel. Children with this type have an aversion to useless systems that only stifle people. It can be like a breath of fresh air when a child with the Rebel type decides it's time to do something different. Like deciding to go outside to eat dinner instead of in the dining room, we all could use a new way of doing things now and again.

The child with the Rebel type can be thoughtful and curious. She loves to learn, and asks why things are the way they are often. She may have very strong feelings when she learns about things that are unfair, especially from those in power.

Chapter 7: The Action Types

How can this type be a challenge?

If the child with the Rebel type feels that teachers or parents are unfair, she will refuse to do what she's told. If she is pushed into following unfair rules, she will find another way to rebel. It can be exhausting to parents when their child is always looking for something to rebel against, especially if the system or rule is healthy and fair.

Okay, so now what do I do?

Once a parent understands the value of this type and appreciates that these children are really trying to make things better, not harder, then a parent can make steps toward common ground. Like negotiating an uprising, there are often places where the parent can give a little. Parents may worry that once they give in, the Rebel child will become even more persistent. If standing firm in their methods has led to a tug-o-war, then loosening the rope a little gives parents less resistance from the other side.

The child with the Rebel type who is pushing for change needs to be heard first. Parents should take the time to hear out the child who refuses to follow the system. For example, the child may not like to go to her room to do her homework right after school. She may think she needs a break, a snack, and the chance to do it in the dining room.

A parent may think it's impossible because the diner is cooking, the TV is on, and delaying homework time will send the message that it's not that important.

If the parent can keep the discussion going, with both explaining their concern and listening to new suggestions from the child, and even trying them now and again, then the child is learning an essential skill. Thoughtful negotiating is so powerful. It truly helps establish healthy, fair change. Without it, there are only dissention and disagreement. It is essential for this type to learn how to negotiate and discuss options.

One important element of this type is that all Rebels initially think that problems are completely unfixable and a complete overhaul is needed. They tend to want to "throw the baby out with the bath water." It's not in their nature to consider that a middle ground even exists. This can be exasperating to parents who are trying to give a little. The Rebel can be very narrow-minded.

During discussions, it's important to keep asking the child to come up with more solutions and not to give up. If the Rebel type can think of any way that satisfies both parent and child, she will have complete dedication to the end result.

How to be with this type:

Many children with this type will grow into frustrated adults if they don't learn the skill of give and take. All they know is that the system isn't working, so it must change. They can learn how to create change that serves everyone if a wise adult can show them how.

Look for ways to let the Rebel do things differently. She'll have her own path, and no one will be able to dissuade her from it. She can bring refreshing new experiences and relieve us of the habits that keep us stuck in the same old routine. Although the Rebel can be challenging at times, with the right guidance she can learn how to institute healthy change.

Detective/Spy

He's nosy and sneaky, and asks a lot of questions.

Is this your child?

He has great intuition and people skills. He can talk to anyone easily. He'll ask questions and is truly curious about others. He may like to hide things or poke in other people's personal items. He loves to know secrets and will work hard to find out the secrets that people know.

What brings out the best in this type?

He will enjoy listening to stories about people. He likes to hear the gossip. He doesn't spread gossip to others too much; he just wants to know about it. He's fun to have at social gatherings because he's curious and a good listener.

He likes know why people behave as they do, especially if someone does something inappropriate. In fact, if something happens at a party, like an argument, the child with the Detective will have seen it and ask about it. Parents of a Detective often say that he "doesn't miss anything."

How can this type be a challenge?

The Detective can be very sneaky—and not for a good reason, either. He will try to sneak anything just for the thrill of getting away with it. Sneakiness is part of this type so completely that no parenting tactic will stop it.

Family Types

He may sneak candy or soft drinks if they are not allowed. He may sneak and play video games. It can get worse if parents think they can stop it. If parents decide the sneaking must stop, they have an impossible task on their hands.

The Detective is also nosy. He'll ask a lot of questions, and that can be tiresome. Even worse, he'll eventually ask a lot of personal questions that can be surprising for adults. The more the adult refuses to answer the questions, the more curious and persistent the Detective becomes. It can feel like the child is invading his parents' privacy, and he is.

Okay, so now what do I do?

The child with the Detective type can take you off guard with his inquiring mind. Once you've gained your senses, he needs to be told that his questions are interesting but not appropriate to answer. If an adult becomes flustered and defensive, the Detective will think there's good information to be found. If the adult can seem polite but bored, the child will lose interest.

At a later date, parents can explain to the child with the Detective that asking too many questions about matters that are inappropriate is unacceptable and will make someone uncomfortable. Even a parent has the right to privacy.

When the child with the Detective type becomes a sneak, it can be a chance to play sneak games with him instead of reprimanding him. If a parent discovers a stash of candy, perhaps the candy can be left just as it is, but later on the parent casually mentions she knows all about it. In fact, she's known all about it for a while, and there's nothing sneaky happening at all.

The most important thing is not removing the items, but removing the allure. The child returns to see the candy still there, but it loses its fun factor. If the parent says that she

Chapter 7: The Action Types

knows all about other items as well and remains unimpressed, then most any hidden treasures will seem less exciting.

This can be difficult if the child has hidden a treasured item, but staying calm and cool is essential to not building the allure. Adding a consequence without delay or fury will take out the fun as well.

If there is no tug-o-war, his rush will be small. The child will still sneak and hide things, but at least he'll begin to learn that there is no benefit. If he's made to feel fear when he sneaks, he will love it even more, and the items he sneaks may become even more risky.

How to be with this type:

The Detective can be a fun and interesting type that can keep you on your toes. And if parents can learn to appreciate the intuition and curiosity of a Detective, they can enjoy this type even more.

Try playing hide-and-seek type games with this child. Stay cool if he does sneaky things, he's trying to get a rush of excitement from you. Help him learn to stay polite with people and avoid getting too personal if people don't like it.

Trust that he can understand family issues early on and try not to keep too many secrets from him. He's a great listener and will be a very understanding person as he matures.

Midas/Miser

**She has entrepreneurial abilities.
She loves to negotiate a valuable exchange.**

Is this your child?

To the child with the Midas, everything has a monetary value; few things are just sentimental. She likes money, both earning it and spending it. She'll trade her toys for other kids' toys if she likes them better. She'll try to talk people out of things they own because she likes them. She'll barter with anything that she thinks others would want.

What brings out the best in this type?

The Midas loves the chance to earn money and purchase things she likes. If she can make money from good grades, she'll work hard at school. If she can earn an allowance for doing her chores, she'll ask to do other chores for more. She'll love getting a piggy bank and monetary gifts for her birthday. From a young age she'll understand the concept of saving for things, and even begin doing so without parental encouragement.

How can this type be a challenge?

The child with the Midas type can seem stingy and even greedy. Her attention is so powerfully aimed at accumulating money and things that she'll have a hard time sharing. She may even hide some of her assets if she thinks others would ask for

Chapter 7: The Action Types

them. She'll likely be fair in her deals and negotiations, but tight-fisted once she's attained the prize.

The Midas also can be closed off when it comes to her personal feelings. She may think she's being generous and open, but compared with others her age she's not. She won't understand that she's protective of herself and her things. To the Midas, any giving feels like a lot and is difficult. Parents may try to convince her otherwise, but she likely won't understand or agree.

Okay, so now what do I do?

Parents often resort to a guilt trip when the child with the Midas (and Miser) type refuses to be generous. Sometimes the child will respond that she didn't ask for much for free, so why should she give much for free? The Midas thinks that she has worked for everything, and so should everyone else. If she is made to give out of guilt, it will only bring out feelings of resentment and confusion.

The Midas has no idea that giving for the sake of giving is a joyful and fulfilling experience. Parents do this for their children, and it is fulfilling until children take it for granted. The child with the Midas knows that gifts can be taken for granted and doesn't want to experience that.

The best way to teach a child about the beauty of giving is to give to others, especially outside the family. When parents model that they have something to share with someone, especially someone who is in need, then the Midas learns that giving is fulfilling.

Most people that have the Midas type are searching for a feeling that is satisfying to their spirit. It is no different with children. Once they learn the art of creating wealth of any kind, they experience a moment of fulfillment, but then they need more. After a while that pattern emerges and could last a lifetime.

Family Types

What could come next is continuing the flow by helping others. It's the natural next step, but it won't be obvious to the Midas unless she has the example to witness.

For example, parents can cook meals for community members who need the help. Include the Midas in the cooking and delivering of the meals, and she will get a feeling of satisfaction that is even greater than earning. This lesson is not about keeping her worth to herself, but rather that with greater worth, more good can be done.

How to be with this type:

Parents can teach the Midas that there is always enough to share by sharing with others. It's important to do more than tithing with a check, or more than putting a few dollars in the basket at church. If parents can find a physical action that helps people in a way that the child can witness and share in doing, she will feel the results of that. Once she experiences the joy of helping others, she will naturally want to experience it again and again. Then no matter how much she makes, and it will likely be a lot, she will continue and share the joy of her wealth.

Chapter 8
The Wild Card Types

Addict

Trickster

Hedonist

Vampire

Don Juan/

Femme Fatale

The Wild Card types can be some of the most challenging archetypes in a family. Nearly all families have at least one of these, and they often are labeled as the "black sheep" of the family. Families can have a type that many members share, like the Addict or Vampire type. It may not be good news to realize that relationship turmoil is from one of these patterns, because it seems like a permanent negative diagnosis.

If you find that family members have a type that is often challenging, even heartbreaking, it's important to take the time to step back and look for the gifts that each of these types can bring. It is better to believe that the more difficult the type, the more powerful the wisdom that comes from it.

By wisdom, I am referring to things like self-discipline, love without judgment, patience, detachment, honesty, and bravery. Living with or even having some of these types will bring out the need for these virtues, but it will also help develop these essential tools for life. These types take work to live with peacefully, but once the keys are found and practiced carefully, the results will be a more harmonious and peaceful family.

Each of these types can be male or female. I've only dedicated a certain gender for ease of reading. The information here is merely an introduction to the type, and upon further exploration an entire book could be written for each. If the reader desires to pursue further study, I recommend that the search include the gifts that each can bring. It is only with compassion and an open heart that we can learn to accept and appreciate the treasures hidden here.

Addict

He has unstoppable focus and desire to do something. He becomes obsessed with things.

Is this your child?

He can be obsessive. Once he sets his attention to something, he will pursue it constantly. He can get very excited about his interest and spend every waking moment doing it. It's not uncommon for the child with the Addict type to love video games. In fact, most people have addict experiences throughout their life. But to have the Addict type as a main type to his personality, the child will display a near-constant desire for some particular thing or experience throughout his life.

He will likely also have a substance that he craves, like sweets or junk food. Even if the substance is removed for a time, once it's reintroduced it will become an obsession again. This is not to say that people who crave certain foods have the Addict type, but if the obsessive nature exists in several areas of his life, he may have this type.

What can bring out the best in this type?

Discipline and development of skill at something are the virtues of having the Addict type. There is so much drive within a child that has this type that, if that drive is channeled in a healthy way, he can become an expert at what he does. He

Chapter 8: The Wild Card Types

can develop strong self-discipline if he's taught that he must pace himself and stay balanced with his interests. It will be extremely difficult for him to stay balanced, but like lifting a heavier weight in order to gain muscle, he'll gain endurance and strength.

If the child with the Addict type has an interest in something healthy, like in the world of fitness or creativity, he can develop skills that can take him far in life. Although the Addict type may grow to become a workaholic, which is not a healthy expression, it's important to recognize that he can achieve many good things with that drive.

How can this type be a challenge?

The moment the Addict becomes so obsessed with something that it undermines his health is the moment the addiction is out of control. Although many of us do things that are not perfect for our health, the Addict will travel much further down the road before he will stop.

For example, kids may stay up half the night playing a new video game. They may do this for a few days even. However, the child with the Addict type will have a constant habit of losing sleep in order to fulfill his desire. Even after the newness has worn off of the game, the Addict will keep obsessing or beg for another new game.

Left to their own, children will stay up late, eat junk food, and avoid the requirements of a healthy life, but most children will follow the guidance of structure and rules that help keep them balanced. Not the Addict. The child with the Addict type will keep looking for ways to get those feelings of excitement and pleasure even if there is a physical cost.

When parents see that the child is not taking care of himself, we often step in and push to get him to do what he needs. Living with a child who obsesses is absolutely exhausting for

Family Types

parents. It's like constantly playing tug-o-war with the child. There is no joy in this scenario.

Okay, so now what do I do?

In our desire to save the Addict type from himself, we take on the role of self-discipline. Parents are his internal moderator from the time he was born, but because he won't develop it like most other children, we keep doing it for him. Instinctually parents know he will fail if left to his own devices, so we take away the computer games, or chocolate, or whatever he's obsessive about. But it's not long before another obsession replaces it.

He will never learn to live more balanced unless he falls and picks himself up.

It's like watching a baby learn to walk. We help him for a time, but there comes a day when we must let him go through the motions of falling, getting up, falling and getting up. Even though parents know this, as he matures, the falls will be more and more unbearable to watch. That's exactly what it takes.

It's imperative that the child with the Addict type experience the pain that his obsession brings. That pain can take many forms, from exhaustion to missing out on other fun or extra work somewhere else. If parents use guilt as a consequence, it is detrimental to the Addicts' self-worth. If a child with the Addict type develops true self-worth, he won't let himself become controlled by his obsessions. By using natural and difficult consequences as a response to his overindulgence, parents can help him grow his desire for balance.

For example, a child with the Addict type stays up to read or play video games most of the night. Even on a school night, he just can't stop and go to bed. Or, he'll wake after a few hours and read or play until sunrise. The next day he's exhausted and struggles through school. He takes a nap in the afternoon,

Chapter 8: The Wild Card Types

barely completes his homework, and stays up again the next night.

His parents take away the object of his affection, and it helps—until another one takes its place.

Perhaps a better response is to leave the child to the consequences of his actions, but "up" the consequences so he'll feel everything that it cost him. Parents could tell him he's allowed to stay up and read or play as long as he likes, but he cannot nap the next day. He has to keep his grades up and be pleasant with all family members. Since he's old enough to decide his bedtime, he's old enough to do a few extra chores, perhaps cleaning the kitchen. He can't go to bed too early, either, to make up for missing sleep, because he has to be part of the family.

If he can complete all of these requirements, like any adult would, he is welcomed to read or play all he wants. If he doesn't follow these rules, he loses the object of his obsession for many months, or permanently.

Instead of merely losing his games or books because his parents decided to take them away, he is completely responsible for maintaining balance in his life in order to keep them.

It's also imperative to have the Addict's life filled with a variety of experiences. The child with the Addict type should have places to go and things to do, and not too much time to just lounge around. While everyone needs some time to relax, too much idle time will drive his desire for the thrill of his obsession. If he has friends, sports, family trips, and activities to attend, he'll naturally have less desire for his obsession.

How to be with this type:

Conversations about the child's obsessions and imbalanced choices will be part of his upbringing, but it's imperative that the child with the Addict type recognize that benefits come

Family Types

with passion and drive. Remind him that whatever goals he sets his mind and attention to, he will likely find success because he's so driven. If he begins to develop dreams and goals that feed his passion for success and achievement, he'll likely learn that balance is easier.

Consecutively, if the child with the Addict type can learn that when he shares his attention and passions with other people, it will bring him companionship, he will be less likely to become isolated and lonely. If he can experience the sweetness of connection with others, and the self-respect that develops from discipline and balance, he can likely avoid the worst patterns of addiction.

Trickster

**She's smart and funny.
She's able to surprise people and loves a big reaction.
She likes to make trouble with people, just for the thrill
of getting them going.**

Is this your child?

She's fun and creative. She likes to see people shocked and stirred up. She'll like to perform magic tricks or do anything that surprises others. She might also be called a troublemaker because she pushes people's buttons. She's very sensitive to the weaknesses in people and may pick on them just to aggravate them.

What can bring out the best in this type?

The child with the Trickster type loves attention. If she can impress people with her talents she'll be happy and entertaining. If she can get into performing in some way, she will be fearless.

If the Trickster is hanging out with family or friends and things are calm and subdued, she will spice things up. She may put on music or play tricks on people just to have fun. The child with the Trickster type is the life of the party.

How can this type be a challenge?

If the Trickster isn't getting the attention she desires, she will make trouble with people just for the thrill of getting them going. She may pick on someone until he is upset and loses his cool. She may say something to embarrass someone just to see

Family Types

his reaction. She can offend people easily and seems to have no sense about being polite in a relationship.

Okay, so now what do I do?

The child with the Trickster type will not realize that her troublemaking is truly hurting other people. She can be very difficult to stop once she's started, because to her it's just a thrill. Because her desire to cause trouble comes from her need for attention, any time she's stirring the pot is a signal that she needs some one-on-one time with a parent. Clearly it's necessary to wait until the troubled moment has passed. Parents shouldn't reward her for her rude behavior.

Once she's stopped, and consequences are given and completed, it would be a good to spend some time doing something personal. Whether it's taking a walk or chatting an extra 20 minutes before bedtime, any opportunity to slow down and hear her talk will help tremendously. The Trickster is always appreciative of her parents' time and attention, and with enough personal moments she will turn her energies to real fun for everyone, not just herself.

How to be with this type:

It may seem that this type is needy, but that's just what it takes. Giving a child extra time and attention has huge rewards in the long run. Leaving her needing more and more will create family disruptions that will cost more in the end. The kind of attention needs to be empathetic and compassionate. It won't fill her up to spend 15 minutes a day getting fussed at.

Either parent can fill this role, and even another relative can help. Some children just need to know that their parents see them and love them before they can be their best self. The Trickster is one of these types. In return she'll fill the family with the kind of fun and surprises that others would envy.

Hedonist

He loves to have a good time.

Is this your child?

He spends most of his time trying to have a good time. The child with the Hedonist type may even try to avoid work unless he can make it fun. He's social and entertaining. He loves the good things in life. While most kids want a video game, the Hedonist wants a whole game room.

What brings out the best in this type?

The Hedonist loves parties, friends, good food, and new toys. If it's time to unwind, the child with the Hedonist type will be the first one there. He can bring out the fun in everyone. His zest for life is contagious. People love to be around him. He's rarely serious, and more playful than anything.

How can this type be a challenge?

The child with the Hedonist type may get so wrapped up in fun and play that he has a hard time settling down for work and rest. Even with a good routine, which is essential, the Hedonist resists bedtime or chores. It can be frustrating for parents that keep structure at home to constantly press their child to do the necessities. The Hedonist has little endurance for the mundane. Even if he's finally settled down to do his homework, he can become weary and restless.

He also has a tendency to go overboard with fun. He may lose sleep because he won't stop playing. He may overindulge in sweets and treats, making himself sick to his stomach. He doesn't have an internal "off switch" that tells him he's had enough.

Okay, so now what do I do?

Although most parenting advice includes giving children structure and discipline, it will be less effective for the child with the Hedonist type. It's still very necessary, but parents shouldn't feel ineffective just because his response isn't like other children's. He will always resist too much structure, but some is essential.

It will be helpful to tell him of his special ability to enjoy life and that his happiness is a blessing to others. If the Hedonist is appreciated, he will feel less guilty about his disposition. As he matures, people may criticize the Hedonist for his lack of desire to do the more mundane chores. It does not necessarily mean he will grow to be lazy. In fact, many Hedonists turn their passionate desire for the good life into a strong work ethic in order to maintain it. In this way he may sacrifice close human connection because he must work so hard for his things.

The most effective life skill for the Hedonist to learn is to take good care of himself by trying to stay balanced. He will never find it to be second nature, but if he is self-aware he will be able to adjust his overindulgences easier. If he knows how good he feels when he's had enough rest he can learn to make time to sleep enough. If he learns that spending time with people is fulfilling, he'll be less likely to use other means to fill himself up.

How to be with this type:

The Hedonist is a treasure to our overworked planet. He

Chapter 8: The Wild Card Types

can remind us of why we are working so hard, which is to have fun. Taking the time to let the child with the Hedonist type lead us in having more fun and pleasure will raise the quality of our lives. Although he will go too far at times, it's important not to shame him, either. Teaching him healthy habits and structure may be especially difficult, but he needs at least a little.

Make sure he is given responsibility and consequences if he doesn't follow through. Since having a good time is so important to him, it would be a good way to reward him when he's completed his homework and chores.

His curiosity and zest for life will make the good times especially fun for the whole family. Let his happy nature infect the way things are done at home. This type can be a great pleasure to have as a child.

Vampire

**She loves to give people her complete attention.
(But she'll need it in return.)**

Is this your child?

She asks lots of questions and is very affectionate, giving lots of hugs. She seems sweet and is genuinely interested in people. She's very friendly with everyone, even her parents' friends. She gets "glued" to anyone who gives her attention but has a hard time letting go. To most people who meet her, she seems especially friendly, but after a while she can become exhausting.

The child with the Vampire type has a lot of trouble feeling good in her own skin. She'll complain of a lot of issues, from bumps and bruises to mean friends and intolerant teachers. Some parents may get calloused from the complaints; others may wish people were more compassionate with their child.

What brings out the best in this type?

The child with the Vampire type is fearless when she meets new people. She'll easily make her impression by talking and asking questions to anyone available. It's lovely to have an affectionate child who bestows her hugs on people generously. She seems to soak up the attention of others, and for people who aren't used to so much attention it is delightful.

Chapter 8: The Wild Card Types

How can this type be a challenge?

The child with the Vampire type can be very needy. She has a hard time keeping herself content and needs outside attention very frequently. She can be precocious and do anything to engage people, even trying to do things to help them that are too difficult for her age. Once she's engaged in conversation and giving, she'll attach herself to the person like he or she is her best friend. It can feel as though she's draining people because she needs so much attention.

In fact, she is draining them. It's because she has a hard time appreciating the good things in herself and struggles to value her gifts. She seems to always need others to do it for her.

It will look like the child with the Vampire type has low self-esteem, and parents could spend a lot of energy trying to make up for an imperfect life. If parents are divorced, the divorce will be blamed for her self-image, but that's not necessarily the root of the issue at all. Even people who are raised in the best environments can have this type. For them, the fact that they "had it all" will be to blame for their neediness. If a child is born with this type, she just has it. The concern for her self-esteem is what has to be dealt with.

Okay, so now what do I do?

The most important thing to teach the child with the Vampire type is boundaries. She will have no clue that she's crossing people's comfort zone and asking too much of them. It may seem that she will never learn this, and she will likely have a hard time understanding it. If it is never pointed out to her, though, she will always wonder why people get tired of her and eventually reject her. This kind of situation is too painful for people of any age, so learning how to empathize

Family Types

and respect the boundaries of others is perhaps her greatest life lesson.

Teaching her about boundaries is also essential because as she matures, she may let people cross her boundaries too often. She'll do this so she can get close to them, but eventually the cost will be too high.

For example, she may give the new girl at school a gift so she feels welcomed. Then she become the girl's best friend, but demands too much attention. The new girl eventually branches out, making new friends, but the child with the Vampire type feels rejected. She'll try to give gifts again in order to retain the friendship, but soon it costs too much to maintain. No one wins in this situation, and the child with the Vampire type really has no clue about how she created it.

If a wise and loving parent can have a conversation about when a friendship takes too much to maintain, and that it's important to take a break, the child may begin to understand when she's pushing too hard for attention. The child with the Vampire type will have this pattern many times over, and that likely can't be stopped, but she can learn to honor the moment things have gone too far, and learn to step away.

Additionally, the child with the Vampire type needs to find a way to see the good things in herself. Finding experiences that give her evidence of her worth is essential. It is always beneficial to someone's worth when they learn to give to someone without expecting a return.

For example, parents can play a kind of secret giving game where the child learns to give to someone and the recipient doesn't know who it was.

How to be with this type:

Some children are just naturally giving this way, and that part of the Vampire cannot be stopped, nor should it. Helping the child learn how it feels when she becomes too needy for a return of attention, or when others take too much of her, will help her begin to take positive action earlier. The better she is at recognizing this pattern in herself and others, the better her relationships will be her whole life.

Don Juan/Femme Fatale

The Don Juan and Femme Fatale make people feel special.

Is this your child?

Both the Don Juan and the Femme Fatale are charming and very good at giving compliments. They will sweet-talk grandparents and teachers, indulging them in praise and admiration. For example, they might tell Grandma that her cookies are the best they ever tasted—and they'll mean it, too—but the very next week that compliment goes to someone else.

What brings out the best in this type?

The Don Juan and the Femme Fatale live in the moment. They enjoy whatever and whoever is in front of them. They are friendly and engaging. They know how to make people feel admired and loved; it's easy and natural for them.

They are often affectionate and giving. Little boys with the Don Juan type love getting attention from the ladies, especially grown ladies. They'll attach themselves to people who they have a particular attraction to and follow them around. The Femme Fatale seems older than her years because she can engage in conversation with people much older than she.

How can this type be a challenge?

The Don Juan and Femme Fatale are so good at getting

Chapter 8: The Wild Card Types

what they want by giving people attention that they begin to believe it's the only way they can get what they want. The Don Juan may want something from his mother, but before he asks, he gives her a compliment as a way to buy her permission. He feels as though he needs to give before he can get. He uses his charms to manipulate instead of just asking outright.

The Femme Fatale may define her worth by how much attention she is given. She feels valuable only when someone is interacting with her, so she may do whatever it takes to get noticed. Without other experiences that fill her self-worth, the child with the Femme Fatale type will begin to think that the only way to be loved is by getting attention.

Okay, so now what do I do?

The boy with the Don Juan type has a great gift of charm that he'll use his whole life, but his parents are in the unique and valuable position to make sure he knows he's loved even without his compliments. Parents also need to make sure he notices that he's giving a compliment in order to get something. With awareness of his tactics, they will be able to decide if his compliment is genuine or meant to achieve something.

One method to help him curb his manipulative compliments is to have him practice asking for something without giving a compliment first. This could be surprisingly difficult for him. For the Don Juan, it is exceptionally painful to be told "no." He'll go great lengths to avoid it. To him it feels like a rejection.

One way to help him raise his ability to handle rejection is to make a game of "no." Tell him to ask for things, crazy big things, like an airplane or a new sports car. Then have him listen to his parent say "no." Over and over he asks for something, over and over he hears "no." If this is done with humor, he will learn that "no" isn't so bad and doesn't have to hurt so much.

The Femme Fatale needs to know that there are many ways

to feel loved, and that she can tap into other life experiences and talents when she feels needy. Wanting to be loved is universal and normal, but the Femme Fatale relies on the attention of others too much for it. If she can learn to love herself by doing things that build self-respect, she will have lasting contentment. One way a girl can learn self-respect is to give and trust her with responsibilities. The more she can depend on her own judgment and work ethic, the more she will build self-confidence. When a girl has self-confidence, she'll need the attention of others less.

How to be with this type:

The Don Juan and Femme Fatale are not destined to a life of constantly seeking the attention of others, unless they are truly neglected. Parents can help them see that they are loved just because. Although they will use their charms often, it isn't cause for concern unless they are unaware that it has become manipulative. They need to learn that people will love them no matter what.

Parents can also remind children with these types that giving attention and compliments is a special talent, but only when it's from the heart.

Part 2

Types for Survival and Self-Esteem

Chapter 9
The Universal Types

Saboteur

Victim/Victor

Sell-Out

There are four types that each one of us has. Everyone, no matter what, will have these four types within their personality spectrum. Although they seem only to be difficult types, Caroline Myss explains in her book *Sacred Contracts* that they are the building blocks of our self- esteem. Without these four archetypes to help us, we would never build healthy self-esteem and self-worth, because none of us is born mature and wise.

The four Universal archetypes are the Saboteur, the Victim, the Sell-Out, and the Child types. Our children must have experiences with each of these four types in order to be able to protect themselves and mature into responsibility and independence. We also refer to these four as our survival archetypes, and how we handle these four will influence our lives more than any of the other types.

Each of these four archetypes holds a key to building personal power, and as parents we can use these as a kind of map to help guide our children in building their self-esteem and self-worth.

Just as learning to walk includes falling and getting back up, the universal archetypes of the Saboteur, Victim, and Sell-Out often feel like stumbling blocks. When we accept that each pattern is part of growing up, we can look for the wisdom in each, without getting trapped in the challenges that each type brings.

What kinds of challenges are associated with the Universal types?

The process of growing up is not limited to just our physical

Family Types

change of size. Maturity of a human being includes learning how to adapt to our environment and interact with other people. The Universal types, which include the Saboteur, Victim, and Sell-Out, each give us experiences that develop our wisdom.

The Saboteur helps us develop endurance to complete a task that otherwise might have been left unfinished because of our nature to avoid change and difficulty.

The Victim teaches us that after someone has crossed our boundaries, leaving us feeling victimized, we can learn to stand up for ourselves and refuse to let it happen again.

The Sell-Out helps us learn what our true values are and avoid selling out our worth in order to fit in with others.

Why are there so many Child types?

The fourth Universal type is the Child. We all begin life as a child, and how we experience our childhood influences many of our decisions even as adults.

The last chapter explains the various Child types and how they may express themselves in children. They include: the Nature Child, the Magical Child, the Eternal Child and the Orphan Child, the Invisible or Perfect Child, the Divine Child, the Wounded Child, and the Adult Child. You will pick one of these per person. If two of them seem just right, still pick only one.

Which types are my child's?

If you are trying to decide what 12 types your child has, include the Victim, the Saboteur, the Sell-Out, and one of the Child types. The remaining eight types will be chosen from the first eight chapters of this book. The 12 types together create a complex and thorough picture of your child. With this picture you can develop an effective an appropriate response to any issues that come up.

Chapter 9: The Universal Types

As parents, we try to protect our kids from so much, whether it is feeling victimized, settling for less than their best, or even fearing what others think of them. We can't possibly believe it's our job to stop all the storms. In fact, the most difficult part of parenting is balancing risk and experience with protection and security. Letting them fail, just enough, sometimes is the wisest thing to do.

When we tell our children that these challenges are part of growing up and that we've gone through them, too, we show them that their power of choice is more important than anything. We can share how we've used the wisdom and come through tough times better than before. Learning the gifts of the Universal types is the key to helping your children develop true self-esteem.

Saboteur

The Saboteur tempts us to quit and give up, yet when we persevere we attain true self-esteem.

What is the Saboteur type?

We all have hopes and dreams. Children create dreams with abandon when they are small. If they are encouraged, they will carry that ability into adulthood. We know that it takes a lot to bring dreams to life; it requires effort and the willingness to change. Yet there are times when we don't feel like persevering and we consider giving up.

Kids need to have some successes and milestones to show for their effort. Without the experience of success, they give up. If they have milestones that are too difficult or too far off, they give up. If they have no downtime or play time, they will get burned out. If they are forced into activities that are not the least bit enjoyable, they will resist doing them. The Saboteur is the perfect type to help us recognize when these issues have come up.

For example, even as I write this chapter I feel like I'd rather go watch a movie with the kids. It would be easier, and more fun, but this chapter would not get written.

The Saboteur type tells us we'd rather not try, to take a break and do the work only when we feel like it. When we listen to the Saboteur we may even believe it's too hard and give up completely. It makes us think we may not have the

Chapter 9: The Universal Types

ability to stick with it because we would rather not miss out on something else.

But if we give our dreams the attention they need in spite of the Saboteur—if we stick to the task—then we build self-esteem of the highest quality. The archetype of the Saboteur is our guide to showing us where we are not yet willing to go the distance, but have the choice to try anyway.

In what ways do my children have the Saboteur?

Let's say your child wants to play a sport or learn a musical instrument. He begs you to let him start lessons, so you make the commitment. You buy the uniform or instrument, pay the fee, and sign him up. Three lessons later, he wants to quit. That's the Saboteur.

There are social Saboteurs. Your child wants to join the Cub Scouts, Brownies, or another school-based group, like cheerleading or debate team. He attends several meetings, and then starts to complain that he doesn't feel like going anymore. The effort it takes to make new friends and become part of a group may seem too difficult to many children.

Sometimes parents are the initiator of the activity, signing their kids up for swim team or football, or maybe art lessons. We have many reasons for doing this, and hopefully our children will respond well to the activity. But sometimes they hate it, even if it's "good for them." They will purposefully sabotage their lessons by goofing off or forgetting important items.

Whining and fussing about going to practice is another way the Saboteur comes out. We can't expect our kids to have the discipline of an adult; that's part of giving them structure and rules. When we find ourselves caught in a tug-o-war, constantly pushing them to finish what they start, we may need to stop and look at why the Saboteur is affecting them so much.

Family Types

Why are kids this way so much?

Often, when a child decides to start lessons or join a club, it is because he has a dream or fantasy about how it will be. Children don't realize how much effort it will take to accomplish the dream. We assume they understand what effort it will take because they seem to have such passion and desire, but they haven't really had enough life experience to understand how challenging things can be. Children are clueless about how quickly something can get boring. They can't imagine all the work because they're only dreaming of how it will be when they've achieved it.

Also, children today are used to quicker and quicker gratification. They think they should be able to learn something almost instantly. With the use of computers and cell phones they can access anybody, anywhere, anytime. Even e-mail is too slow for this generation. Playing a video game has to include quick and impressive rewards or they lose interest. Even learning a musical instrument seems to take too long if kids are used to getting the rush of accomplishment from the video game version. They're used to instant gratification, so their expected mental time line to see achievement is faster than reality. Parents have to be prepared to face off with the Saboteur and the effects of the digital age.

Okay, so now what do I do?

Without destroying their excitement, we need to help them define a reasonable timeline that's more in sync with reality. For example, if a child wants piano lessons, before you start lessons, make an agreement with the child about the minimum time and effort she has to put forth.

You can say: "If you want to take piano lessons, let's commit to three months of lessons and 10 minutes of practice, three

Chapter 9: The Universal Types

times a week. After that, we'll see how you're doing, and we'll decide if we need to do more or stop altogether." When a child understands what she agreed to, it makes it easier for her to follow through. Most music teachers suggest at least 15 minutes every day to practice, and that is great advice, except it may be wise to start off with an easier goal and work up to that.

Goals should not be endless, either. We can't sign children up expecting them to go week in and week out for months or years until they can play like a pro. They need something to look forward to other than the fantasy in their head. Perhaps the music teacher can help set an easy goal that makes sense for the first few months. Often teachers already know what to start working toward, and it's just a matter of everyone getting clear about it.

Once a child knows what can be done, and in a relatively brief amount of time, she will be able to recognize when she's accomplished it. The satisfaction that comes with accomplishment is so powerful the Saboteur will all but disappear. If the child has enjoyed the process so far, she'll likely be able to increase her commitment and goal.

On the other hand, if a child really finds the lessons unbearable even after she accomplishes the goal, then the lessons may not be worth the time and money at all. The Saboteur can help us see what we don't want just as much as anything else. That information is essential to accept. We aren't born to do everything; even when we have tons of talent and ability in something, we may not have the passion.

As parents we want our children to feel as fulfilled as possible in their adult lives. One way to attain that is to help them learn to listen to the guidance within them. The Saboteur can help them understand what they truly are called to do. If they have their goals organized and accomplished, yet still feel disinterested, it may be time to take a break and wait for fresh inspiration.

One more possibility, especially with children, is that sometimes there are small issues that sabotage their interest in something. For example, are the lighting and environment that the child has to practice in good? Are they comfortable enough to sit long enough to practice? Dangling their feet from a seat that is too high for young children can be more uncomfortable than we realize. Are there distractions that make practice time seem like no fun? Is the TV on, or are other kids allowed to play within sight, or is the space messy? These small issues can make a big difference in whether or not children feel like practicing. It's worth a little time to assess the situation before proclaiming the child has given up and the Saboteur has won.

What do I do when he says it's too much work?

Sometimes the Saboteur shows up when kids get lost in the labor of learning and lose touch with their original dream. Before you decide to start the lessons, ask your child what he hopes to get from the lessons. What does he imagine he'll experience when he learns his new skill? Taking time to ask, and even write down, what the dream means can be an effective resource when the child feels lost in the chore of learning. If you can give back to him his own words and feelings, it could reignite his desire and passion.

I've often seen people create a dream board or poster with cut-out words or pictures of what the dream will feel like when they reach it. If a child can see a daily reminder of what she has chosen to do, and what it will feel like when she is living it, she will have a much easier time staying on course.

Sometimes kids feel like it will take forever to live their dream. The dream is still great, but they worry they'll be old by

Chapter 9: The Universal Types

the time it happens. Help them plan a short-term goal so they can experience at least some of their dream.

For example, my son started taking drumming at 8 years old, thinking one day he could be in a band. He enjoyed the lessons, but didn't have a place to show off what he was learning. He asked why he should continue to take drumming if he wasn't playing in front of people. I offered to take some video of him playing and put it on a DVD for his grandparents to see. He loved the idea, and his teacher arranged for him to learn a few solos. He seemed happier to practice after this.

Then, when school started again, he signed up to be in the school band as a drummer. He knew the school band performed at several events. Because he had so much experience, he was put with the advanced students, which further helped him see some results. He's proud of his accomplishments, and now he has several opportunities a year to live some version of his dream.

Most people need positive feedback from "the crowd" at some point or the work will feel like it's in vain. When the Saboteur is talking, it's time to listen. Often it will be the voice that helps us propel further and faster than we thought we could.

What about when we sign up our kids for an activity and they don't like it?

It's like making kids eat their veggies: It's good for them, but they fuss and fight. Many kids are placed in sports or other activities that they may not enjoy, but that bring them good health and much-needed exercise. As a former personal trainer, I know exercise is critical to a long, healthy life, and with childhood obesity skyrocketing we simply can't let our kids off the hook with this one. If you decided your kids must do a sport, and they don't like it, or they don't like sports at all,

Family Types

creating a family culture that includes exercise is essential. A family culture is something that your whole family agrees upon that everyone supports. Does your family brush their teeth every day? That's part of your culture. Of course, anything that's just a chore with no apparent award is a bummer. It's easy to teach kids that they'll get a cavity if they don't brush, but what is the payoff for exercise or some other useful activity?

First, address family culture. State clearly that as a family you all get enough sleep, eat healthy food, go to work and school, and exercise. Exercise is as important as brushing your teeth. Tie in the health benefit of the activity. Announcing the family values with no apologies is powerful to children. They listen and believe concrete statements. If you repeat it regularly, they will probably believe it forever.

By the way, we can't expect our children to do more than we are willing to do. When exercise and eating well are part of our family culture, it means we do it, too. If we don't do for ourselves, what can we expect them to do? We can announce our beliefs all day and they'll see right through it.

Second, establish the payoff. This is only if the children really don't like the activity. When kids love an activity, the activity is the reward. If children must do something that they don't like, a reward for the effort will help them avoid becoming resentful. Just like going to bed on time, it may feel like missing out, but we're all rewarded with a refreshed mind and body the next day. How can you show them the benefits of exercise if they don't yet see or feel the results?

Step back and look at what habits you're instilling that they can take into adulthood. If they spend their entire childhood as active people, it will feel normal when they are adults. So even if you have to use an alternate motivator, the long-term result is an active adult who feels happy to reward himself.

By far, the best reward is social connection. It may just be a few minutes, but tying work with human connection makes work feel like a path to contentment. It may be having dinner together, talking together, or planning the weekend activities. Endorphins after exercising are higher than before. The hour or so after children attend a practice for sports is the perfect time to connect as a family.

How to appreciate this type:

It's important to realize that we all have the Saboteur, and we will each experience times when we want to quit because it's getting too hard. Any child who feels like quitting is really normal. It's common issue for all people. It definitely doesn't reflect our parenting, or that we have a lazy child. But it does reflect a need to be clear both up-front and throughout the activities.

The Saboteur in each of us is not meant to stop us from our dreams, but rather push us toward the best expression of them. Discipline doesn't come from forcing ourselves, but rather discovering how to reach our goals with passion and desire. Our children don't know how to create a clear vision. As parents, we can help them learn how to do that. When they are grown they will be equipped to make all their dreams come true.

Victim/Victor

Teaches us how to stand up for ourselves after our boundaries have been crossed.

Why do we all have a Victim?

As a parent we never want our kids to become victimized in any way. The Victim type and experiences that make us feel victimized are part of growing up. Experiences that victimize us may include being bullied or simply mistreated. It includes experiences that seem unjust or unfair, and also the times we are physically or emotionally injured. The events that cause disappointment and even humiliation are part of the Victim experience.

Everyone will have at least some Victim type experiences in a lifetime, but they are not meant to simply hurt us. While no one should invite or wish for these painful moments, their use in our growth is unquestionably one of the most powerful. Our children will have trials and, although we will do our best to guide them around life's pitfalls, a good parent knows that some lessons must be experienced before they are learned.

What can we gain from the Victim type experiences?

The benefits that can be gleaned from Victim experiences are learning true self-esteem and self-worth. They include the ability to stand up for ourselves and to refuse to allow someone to hurt us. They help us develop the capacity to trust ourselves, our instincts, and our values. Only after we are hurt can we learn to forgive and let go of resentment. Also we can develop concern and empathy for others when we've come through a victim experience.

Although most children develop the capacity to be kind and sensitive by the time they are in school, the strength of that skill will be very weak unless it has been tested. At best, we can give our children guidelines, rules, and structures to use as they grow up. Lessons such as sharing, kindness, patience, and self-control can be drilled into them and yield a healthy-looking result.

Children will inevitably fail to use these skills at some point—and that's exactly what is necessary in order for them to really understand the importance of those lessons.

Learning to share comes from wanting what we can't have.

Learning kindness comes from knowing what it feels like to be left out.

Learning patience comes from being pressured to go faster than we're able to go.

Learning self-control comes from feeling remorseful after we haven't been in control.

Each of these experiences begins with the Victim, and each can end with and important lesson that builds our virtues.

What about the times when my child is truly victimized?

Anytime our kids let someone cross their boundaries, they will get a feeling of anger, sadness, or self-pity. Crossing boundaries may mean anything from someone talking them out of their dessert, someone borrowing a toy and not returning it, or letting someone cut in line at school when they won't do the same in return. It also includes being bullied, beaten, or worse. From the smallest incident to the most painful, these experiences all encompass the Victim type.

Family Types

Every one of these experiences holds the capacity to help our children become the embodiment of healthy self-esteem.

It is completely counterintuitive for parents to instantly accept that a Victim experience can be "good" for their child. It's supposed to feel wrong. Parents are primarily guardians of a child's well-being, and Victim experiences should never feel like a good thing. They aren't.

At some point, though, after the experience is over, parents can begin to look for the gift that comes out of a Victim trial. How long that takes will depend on the situation, but unconditionally and in every incidence there is something to be learned. While we will never wish or want for the Victim experience, it still holds the capacity to transform us in a remarkable way.

Often people will say that they had no idea how strong they were (or their child was) until after they endured a difficult event. Recognizing the virtue of strength is a good place to begin, but to truly glean the gifts available we need to keep looking. Something sweeter and more powerful may be developing. If a parent can also be the guide for the child to find the gifts from the experience, children may learn more than we dreamed.

The gifts that come out of the worst Victim experiences could be courage, fortitude, a renewed belief in personal values, and the creativity to begin a completely different kind of life. These are huge virtues that may not have otherwise been developed. Often, the worse the initial situation, the more powerful the wisdom that can come from it. If a child learns courage, for example, how much better will his adulthood be when he is faced with situations that require it?

True self-esteem comes from self-respect. Self-respect develops from the capacity to forgive. And the ability to forgive comes from learning that we have a choice to move on and take only the gifts from a terrible situation.

Chapter 9: The Universal Types

How does the Victim type come out in my child?

When our kids say that something is unfair, it means they feel victimized. If a child seeks revenge for something, it's the Victim at work. If a child is accused of something, he will likely feel victimized, even if he did the act. Getting caught doing something wrong gives him the same feeling.

The Victim will be a large part of a child's life and, although it is likely to bring the most suffering, it is essential to go through. With better understanding of this pattern, and with wise parenting, children can learn the tools it takes to get through the pain and transform it into wisdom.

Without understanding this essential type, the patterns of victimization will keep repeating. As long as the lessons aren't learned, the pattern will become more frequent. Even worse, there will be less time for relief in between events, creating a sense of nonstop discomfort and even sadness.

We cannot stop all difficult events from affecting our children. We shouldn't, either. If we can help them glean the value from them, they will not only learn strength and endurance, but also the Victor side of this type. The ability to stand up for themselves and forgive others is by far the most powerful tool in any person's life.

What kind of wisdom will my child need to learn?

With smaller issues, our kids can learn to speak up for themselves, act with kindness and patience, and use self-control. Having self-confidence or not will make the largest impact on their ability to succeed as adults. We want our sons and daughters to be able to say "no" when they are pressured to do something that crosses their boundaries of safety. When a small infraction happens, try to put them in the driver's seat of speaking up for themselves.

For example, when they are small, if another child takes a toy from them, encourage your child to ask for it back. Most parents will ask for it themselves, and as a model that's fine. At some point, though, the child needs to do it alone. When children can speak up for themselves they'll be able to learn self-respect.

Another issue that children face is when things don't feel fair. Most parents know that the "fair" word is lopsided for children. It's normal for kids to feel like they should win all the time. Young children haven't learned empathy yet, so it seems normal for them that things should always go their way, no matter how others are affected. While we can't expect children to grow up overnight, this period is a great example of how children will feel victimized even when things are perfectly fair. It helps them learn empathy. In the natural order of life, this is healthy.

It's only when children are "spoiled" during adolescence that this issue can become unhealthy. A child who never endures the feelings of unfairness can't develop concern for others. In the same way, a child who truly has an unfair and tortured adolescence is at risk for having little or no self-worth. Balance is essential.

What if my child is a "crybaby" and always asking for attention?

There are some kids that find "playing the victim" to be useful to get attention. The child who is always "getting hurt" and needing a band-aid falls into this category. Parents may feel that they are constantly dealing with a hurt or needy child. The more the child feigns injury, the less the parent wants to show concern. It will feel like the child is sucking energy and never satisfied.

Most parents can recognize a need for attention when this

Chapter 9: The Universal Types

behavior begins. Most parents don't want to feed it, so they'll avoid giving it attention. The remedy can't stop there.

Giving attention to children when they're playing victim is like feeding them candy when they're hungry. It's a quick fix that leaves them even hungrier down the road. They need truly satisfying attention, and one way to give them that is discovering what their other types need.

When parents discover the other parts of their children's personalities, they discover other ways to connect and appreciate them. When a child is seen for all that he is, and when he's accepted and loved for exactly who he is, he will feel deeply satisfied. This kind of acceptance will create an environment that is so fulfilling that the Victim craving for attention will all but disappear.

How to appreciate this type:

It's perfectly normal to dread this type, for our children and even for ourselves. When we know that inevitably a Victim experience can help our children become empowered and loving, we can help them begin the process quicker. We don't have to drill it into them. We can, however, model the capacity to stand up for what's right, and forgive others and move on toward a more gentle and compassionate life. That is the Victor side of the Victim.

Sell-Out

The Sell-Out helps us recognize when we sell ourselves short in order to fit in.

What is the Sell-Out?

Children want to fit in. They want to fit in with their families, their school, and their friends. This is normal and healthy, because it means we desire connection with others. The ability to feel connected and part of a community is incredibly important to our health and well-being. It is essential to learn how to develop friendships and maintain relationships with people.

In order to develop healthy relationships, children also need to learn that honoring themselves is just as important. If a child betrays himself in order to fit in with the crowd, he has just experienced the Sell-Out.

An example of a child selling out includes saying the things that others expect him to say. He may like something, maybe a healthy food or a certain football team, but he'll say he doesn't in order be accepted. The Sell-Out can help children fit in, but there will be a price. At some point the price will increase and it will no longer be worth it.

That crucial point is most obvious in tweens (children who are 11 years old or so). At this age, children begin to value their individuality but lack the certainty that they can make it on their own. This is like a meeting of two rivers. There is a collision of forces that haven't yet decided which way to go.

Chapter 9: The Universal Types

Although young children can begin to wrestle with issues surrounding their values, the fact that they are still very connected to their family keeps them from becoming too upset for long.

Tweens, on the other hand, are starting to pull away from their family. This is healthy and normal. We want our children to desire independence; otherwise they would not grow and "leave the nest."

At the same time tweens are pulling away from family, they are also gathering new relationships in the form of friends. Tweens will pressure each other to agree in order to feel like they belong together. This is when the struggles of the Sell-Out begin to grow.

In what ways do children Sell-Out?

Each of us is born with a sort of internal gauge that tells us whether or not something is okay or not okay. It tells us whether something is good or bad, and it even tells us if we like or dislike something. In young children and teens it is an incomplete gauge, because children haven't experienced very much of life yet. And although there are some things children may be ambivalent about, there are far more things that children are sure of.

For example, if a child's internal gauge says that they do not like making fun of others, yet their friends are doing it, the child will experience a feeling of discomfort. This is the moment that is necessary for a child to encounter in order for him to develop the capacity to honor himself. The moment he "sells out" and joins in the crowd in talking about others, he'll feel both better because he fit in and worse because he betrayed himself. This is one of the reasons the tween years are so difficult. The constant collision of forces is very challenging.

Parents know that children need good friends, but what

Family Types

that means is that children need friends who are similar in their value system. The drive for independence to grow up and leave the family, coupled with a set of friends that have different values, can create a destructive combination.

What can a parent do when the Sell-Out is "out of control"?

Permissive parenting won't help this situation. The internal gauge of a person is begun well before birth. We are born with much more than our disposition and temperament. As the first part of this book shows, children are born with preferences and values that are extremely ingrained well before birth. Simply letting children "stretch their wings" in order to calm the clashing rivers will not be enough. In fact, it may prove dangerous if a child doesn't learn that it's his values that must be honored, not just independence.

When children are in the midst of selling out, they may not realize that they are selling out who they really are. They will often lash out at parents for being too controlling because that's where it all began. They desired independence, they became closer to their friends, they ended up betraying themselves, and the pain of that is blamed on the thing they wanted to be free of.

If parents can see that the desire to leave the nest is normal, and the true issue is a lack of new connections that are in line with the child's values, then parents may be able to head off or tame the issues. The most important thing to focus on is helping the child find friends who are in line with his values. It doesn't have to be the friends he spends most time with, although that is ideal. If a child is experiencing the internal clash of independence, he needs someone to connect with outside of his family, and that someone must share his values.

Once a child experiences the peaceful feeling that comes from a relationship outside of the family, it is easier for him to recognize what he needs deep down. At that point it will be much easier for him to find more of these connections.

So where does a family fit in to this?

Learning healthy independence is only the first step for a child. Ideally, a child will break away from the family only as much as it takes for him to learn to take care of himself and follow his values. Hopefully our children will learn that family is a source of love and support no matter what phase they are in.

The next phase (which may develop at the same time as independence) is interdependence. I've taken this word from modern psychology to describe people who have the ability to honor and take care of themselves, and also to honor and care for their family and friends. Help your child learn that growing up doesn't mean abandoning the family altogether, but rather including them as part of his life.

Most children will believe both are not possible. Kids see things as black or white, and the desire to get out on their own can be all-encompassing. Children and teens will learn the concept of interdependence easier if they have parents who see and accept all that they are. It is a positive force that will be difficult to push away.

Letting a child learn what it feels like to sell out, and also what it feels like to honor themselves, will enable him to desire relationships that are strong and healthy. We all need friends that love and accept us for who we are, no matter what our differences. A family that embodies that is a powerful example that each of us should have.

Chapter 10
The Child Types

Nature Child

Invisible/Perfect Child

Magical Child

Divine Child

Eternal Child

Wounded Child

Orphan Child

Adult Child

The fourth survival and Universal type you will choose is one of the Child types. Each of us has experienced childhood, but the thoughts and beliefs we developed are reflective in the archetype we were born with. It can be difficult to choose which type your child is, because we experience at least a little bit of all of them.

We've all felt like the Magical Child at some point, willing to believe anything is possible. Most of us have felt a connection to nature and animals like the Nature Child. We've each felt, at some point, unnoticed, like the Invisible Child.

By the time we reach adolescence we will have one or two patterns that are more frequent. Narrow down the possibility as much as you can. If you are torn between two, pick one to work with first. Uncovering the gifts and challenges of that Child archetype will be very rewarding. The second Child archetype can be useful to add depth to your understanding but should be treated as an aside, not as one of the 12 core types we use in this work.

Discovering your children's 12 most influential archetypes is a powerful tool in helping them become all they're meant to be. Recognizing when a type is expressing itself and responding compassionately are two of the most loving and validating gifts we can give our children.

Any of these types can be a boy or girl. I use gender to make reading about them easier, but I don't see any type as exclusive to males or females. Remember that these are not so much literal as they are qualities and patterns. The more frequent the pattern, the more likely the fit.

Nature Child

She has a deep connection to animals, nature, and the environment.

Is this your child?

She loves animals. She'll love getting new pets. She'll spend time with her new pets and not lose interest after a few weeks like most other children will. She'll also love the outdoors, and enjoy taking walks or bringing her toys out to play.

What brings out the best in this type?

A Nature Child is most content with a pet. Even if parents don't enjoy the responsibility of owning a pet, it's worth the extra effort to get one because the Nature Child will spend many happy hours tending to it.

If a Nature Child can't have a pet, she'll be happiest outside playing. She will feel rejuvenated and enlivened through nature, spending time in gardens and parks. She will feel most at home outside.

How can this type be a challenge?

The Nature Child is usually very sensitive and tender. Because of this, she may feel vulnerable, and in order to feel safe she may have a tendency to be cruel to animals. It can be very disconcerting to parents when a young child is rough to a beloved pet. She may hug it too tight or do something that makes the animal uncomfortable.

This will seem odd, because most of the time a Nature Child is so nurturing and gentle, but if there are any situations that make the Nature Child scared or nervous she may seek a way to manage those feelings by treating her pets aggressively. It's a way to feel in control of something.

Okay, so now what do I do?

The worst thing a parent can do is make the child feel ashamed. Although it is an automatic and understandable reaction to respond strongly, it won't address the root of the problem. Of course, parents need to remove the vulnerable pet immediately from the child's vicinity.

Once that's done, an age-appropriate conversation should be had about what the child is doing. Most times children don't really know why they are doing it. Kids usually can't articulate feelings nor connect behavior to uncomfortable feelings. Speaking to them about feeling upset or worried and then handling a pet aggressively will help them connect the feelings with the behavior.

We can't always protect children from feelings that are uncomfortable or worse, but we can teach them proactive ways to handle those feelings. Sometimes we just need to tell them that we know they're feeling upset and we're available to be with them.

Just making the connection may not be enough to stop the automatic behavior. Punishing the child may only create more feelings of shame and anger. If a child can learn that she is in control of the pet in a responsible way, the urge to hurt it will dissipate.

It's amazing how effective giving a child responsibility can be. Most feelings of sadness and fear that children have stem from helplessness. We are all born helpless and eventually become self-sufficient. Children are in between those periods, and most negative behaviors in children stem from feeling helpless and having the desire to feel self-sufficient. When we give our children a job, or responsibility, we are helping them develop self-sufficiency. We are also helping to eliminate the helpless feelings.

For example, a young child is cradling a pet, but rocking it too aggressively. The pet is okay, but not comfortable. This is clearly not okay. The child won't stop when told, so the parent takes away the animal. The parent can explain that she understands the child may be feeling upset about something, but that treating animals in that way is not okay. Next, the parent explains that the child will not be allowed to play with the pet if she does that behavior.

Once the child is calm and the issue has passed, it is time to give her a job involving the pet. The job should be age-appropriate, but a little difficult. It may be feeding or cleaning the pet or the cage—anything important to maintenance and care. If the child has an important role in the pet's well-being, she'll actually become protective of it. Taking ownership and responsibility of something usually helps develop an attachment and a sense of control. When the Nature Child feels in control, she feels more empowered.

How to be with this type:

The Nature Child is one of the easiest types to live with, especially if there are animals around for her to care for. Children often push parents to take the lion's share of responsibility, but it is essential that a Nature Child learn to care for and nurture the animals in her life.

Each of us will have to deal with power issues. It's the way

Chapter 10: The Child Types

life is and what helps us develop self-esteem. The Nature Child is often a beautiful example of the best in human nature, but if she takes her fears out on her pets, it's a sign that she needs to be in charge of more. The most empowering response a parent can give when our kids feel powerless and mean is to give them more responsibility. It may seem counterintuitive at first, but the more responsibility they can take for the well-being of something, the more empowered they become.

Invisible/Perfect Child

She receives less attention than others because she's often quiet and calm, but at some point she will do whatever it takes to get attention.

Is this your child?

The Invisible Child feels unnoticed compared with her siblings. She may be the middle child, or the one who doesn't need as much attention. To her, everyone else seems special, while she is just plain. She may want to be noticed and do things to show off. She may be a perfectionist and try to gain attention by trying to be perfect. If parents value achievement, an Invisible Child may set an unreachable standard. Sometimes we call this the Perfect Child. Perfection is a symptom of the feeling she has less than everyone else.

Parents may think this is ridiculous, because to us every one of our children is precious. This type thinks she's not noticed, even though it may just be from her perspective. To the Invisible Child, other siblings get more attention. If this child is an only child, then there may be other "issues" that take attention away from her. For example, if a family member is chronically sick or if parents are absent, she may feel invisible.

What brings out the best in this type?

She won't likely be the troublemaker in the family. In fact, she'll be the "easy" one. The Invisible Child will be the rock and

Chapter 10: The Child Types

support for her family. If she finds a way to feel special, she'll likely repeat it over and over. Although her desire to please is very strong, it's because she feels like it's never enough.

She may enjoy getting out and in front of people to perform in some way. She may think that people "see" her when she's on stage so she may pursue an interest in performance. She may love making videos for the Web, or making her friends act in her plays for people to watch.

The Invisible Child likes to make sure that what she does is perfect. She's an achiever with anything she sets her mind to. Her high standard will be very useful as she matures into adulthood. Although her work may seem never good enough to her, she will be dependable to give things her all.

How can this type be a challenge?

Because she has such high standards in order to be good enough, she'll have a hard time accepting excellence instead of perfection. To the Invisible and Perfect Child, anything less than perfect will leave her invisible to others. Although this isn't true at all, this is a value that she was born with; she will always struggle to accept that things are good enough.

The Invisible Child may not make too much trouble while she is very young because she is often quiet. Usually the only time parents begin to worry is during adolescence when an awkwardness and lack of self-confidence become apparent. The Invisible Child isn't comfortable in her skin and may seem shy. She may have a hard time developing the ability to interact with her peers. Parents often wonder if she'll grow out of it.

The good news is she probably will grow out of some of it. All Invisible Children want to be seen and loved, and if they have the benefit of wise parents they will bud into something wonderful. If showmanship and performance become her methods of seeking attention, they can be fun and rewarding.

Family Types

As long as she is aware that at least some of her drive comes from that desire. Children who must be the center of attention can be exhausting to friends and relatives. A little extra attention in other areas may be needed.

Okay, so now what do I do?

The child feeling invisible is not to be blamed on parents or circumstances. In fact, there is no blame for anyone. Everyone's life has challenges, and each of us decides, often subconsciously, how to interpret events. No two people will live the same life, because each of us has our own take on the same events. Similarly, parents can't force a child to feel visible, and we can't take this type out of her. We can recognize that she has it, though, and address it with understanding and compassion.

It may not make sense at first, but each type is born with a kind of fate. The Invisible Child will find a situation that overshadows her and makes her interpret life this way. Something will happen, or she will simply be born with siblings who need attention. It could even be a wonderful event that everyone in the family is involved with, but this child will somehow feel unrecognized.

Our goal as parents is not to try to avoid anything negative and force our children to be happy all the time. Our goal is to help them see first that they have this disposition, and second that they have choices within that disposition.

If a child seems to have the Invisible Child type, it's only necessary for parents to tell her regularly the things that make her feel loved. It means that when parents decide to stop what they are doing and look the child in the eyes and listen, it will mean the world to her.

One-on-one attention in regular doses for the Invisible Child is like sunshine for flowers. Parents who make sure she gets some special care will do much to help build her self-worth.

Chapter 10: The Child Types

The greater challenge with this type comes when she is bent on perfection and torments herself with thoughts of "not good enough." She may struggle with this throughout her life, but if her parents can encourage her to seek excellence, and accept when things aren't perfect, she may find her life to be less stressful. Sometimes just the concept of excellence versus perfection is enlightening enough to help soothe her worries.

How to be with this type:

Taking time to give her undivided attention, words of encouragement, and love is all that's needed to help the Invisible Child on her path. She may want to start performing and that's great. The ability to stand in front of an audience is useful and exciting.

Remind her of all her talents so she doesn't spend too much time doing whatever it takes for attention. Tell her she's loved and appreciated just for being in your life.

Magical Child

She has the ability to believe in miracles again and again, despite disappointments.

Is this your child?

The most profound ability of a Magical Child is to be able to see the good in everything. She has a wonderfully optimistic personality and doesn't feel down for long. If you have had a bad day, she'll try to tell you things that you should feel good about.

She won't spend much time feeling sorry for you, and she doesn't need you to feel sorry for her. She won't complain much—really not much at all. She'll tell you after you've dropped your cup of coffee: "Well Mom, now you can get a fresh one."

What brings out the best in this type?

It won't do much good to try to make this type feel guilty about anything; she just doesn't spend much time feeling down. She's not going to pick on people or get into disagreements at all if she can avoid it. As a female this type won't get involved with adolescent drama. As a male, he won't feel the need to show off and make a scene. The Magical Child is easy-going because she just knows that everything will be okay.

Even when there are bad times, the Magical Child will find the silver lining. Her mottos are "Everything happens for a reason" and "It will be all right in the end." This type is a positive force that can help anyone who needs a good friend.

Chapter 10: The Child Types

How can this type be a challenge?

Even though this type seems to always find contentment, she will still have things in her life that she'd like to change. Her strength in staying positive will be her weakness when it's time to make a stand. Even if something is really important, the Magical Child will have a hard time gathering the strength to make a difference. She won't want to "rock the boat" or put in effort where it's needed. Because of this the Magical Child could end up staying in less-than-ideal situations.

For example, she may have a friend who is beginning to mistreat her. She won't like it and will want it to be different, but she'll make excuses for the person long after it's appropriate. She may end up feeling like a rug, but still tolerate it and find a reason to put up with the relationship.

For all her kindness, the Magical Child doesn't have the drive to change things even when she should.

Okay, so now what do I do?

As a parent of a Magical Child, it's important to appreciate that she is really a gentle spirit and that standing up for herself is one of the hardest things for her to do. This type may need help in this area because it's so unnatural for her to speak up. She may even find it easier to avoid making friends at all.

There are many ways that a parent can teach a Magical Child to change a situation without having to face off with someone. It shouldn't include passive-aggressive behavior, either. Sneaky revenge is not healthy. Instead the Magical Child could make changes in a relationship by beginning to develop new relationships as a means to exit the negative situation. If the child has other friends to turn to, then she won't be stuck with one bad one that she must face. It's easier to make new friends sometimes than change the ones your with.

Another option is having something ready to distract the person who is acting inappropriate. If the Magical Child is dealing with a situation in which someone is sitting near her in class and is picking on her, she will be caught off guard at first. If it continues she may be able to use her powers of positivity to distract the annoying classmate. She could prepare a few topics that would interest the classmate, and, using her sweet and kind disposition, ask the classmate what he thinks. Nothing is more stimulating to an overbearing person than someone listening to him. The classmate will get so wrapped up in himself, he'll forget to pick on someone else.

Although these options don't directly face an aggressor and put an end to it, it may be the better option initially because the Magical Child just doesn't have the stamina to fight for herself. It also gives her options that she can use so she's not backed into a corner. As long as she has choices, she's empowered. At some point, though, she will grow tired of using them. Then she will be able to speak up for herself and put an end to any harassment.

How to be with this type:

The Magical Child is an easy child to parent because she'll help you see the best things in life. With her gentle, easy-going personality she should make friends with no trouble. And as long as she feels like she can maintain self-respect she'll keep her friends for a long time.

When she inevitably has to deal with challenging people, help her find methods that are non-confrontational. Not only will she be able to use them, she'll learn that there are many ways to diffuse people, and those skills will help her throughout her life. Eventually she'll stand up for herself, but it won't be a long and drawn-out drama. This type is a peacemaker. We should all have the sweetness and kindness that the Magical Child brings with her.

Divine Child

He is impressionable and will believe in the values taught to him.

Is this your child?

The Divine Child is similar to Magical Child in that they share a gentle temperament and sweet nature. Where the Magical Child is always simply positive in her assessment, the Divine Child is innocent and impressionable. The Divine Child is easy to influence in matters of morals and values.

A Divine Child is inquisitive and asks many questions. On the other hand, he'll never challenge you about what's true. He'll believe you at your word. He may seem naïve, even as he gets older. Children usually to begin to think for themselves at some point and gain wisdom as they mature, but a Divine Child will look toward authority figures to define his beliefs even into adulthood.

What brings out the best in this type?

The Divine Child had an open mind and is willing to believe anything. It's a delight to parent the kind of person who believes you no matter what. He's willing to accept anything he's taught as truth and will follow without questioning. Raising a trusting child is a delight as long as parents are aware that what they are teaching is permanent.

Family Types

How can this type be a challenge?

When children begin school, inevitably they will have experiences where people will try to take advantage of them or pick on them. It's the nature of people to test each other. The Divine Child won't test other children, which is good, but he won't be able to defend himself either when he's the one tested. His nature is so gentle that he won't have the constitution to stand up for himself. This is not a Victim situation, but rather he will be innocent even to people picking on him.

A good example of this type in our culture is the story of Pinocchio. The child has no idea he's being taken for a ride. It is exasperating to parents that see their child following a leader blindly, and not having the sense to recognize a wolf in sheep's clothing.

Okay, so now what do I do?

It doesn't take much for parents to decide that this type is not able to recognize a negative influence. Parents will likely become overprotective; it's a natural reaction to the weakness that we sense in this type. These children do need a little more protection.

Ideally, though, parents need to find a way for this type to actually experience the consequences of following the wrong leader. Without the knowledge that things may turn out bad, the Divine Child will remain in ignorance.

It will be very hard for parents to do this, because the child will mess up. He will end up in a jam, even blamed for something that he was innocent of. From a young age the child and parent will be thrust into situations in which, if allowed, the child will end up in some kind of trouble. It will be small kinds of trouble when the child is little, and the trouble will get bigger as he matures. It's better to let him learn while he's small.

Chapter 10: The Child Types

This doesn't mean throw him to the sharks (for Pinocchio, it was a whale) and let him end up in a truly bad situation that will leave him scarred. It *does* mean, whenever possible, letting him feel the consequences of following someone and not thinking for himself. This may feel unnatural for parents, but if we can recognize that this type won't learn to protect himself and think for himself, until he's felt the consequences of it, then we can endure watching the inevitable.

How to be with this type:

As parents of a Divine Child we have to be careful not to become overprotective. We can feel how fragile and naïve this type is, and we will want to keep him that way. The fallout, though, from a childhood without challenges is that this type will be unprepared for adult life.

Parents should also avoid complete abandonment and neglect. This type will not fare well without some kind of protection. It's best to advise the child and then step back. In this way the child has the benefit of good council, a loving and caring parent, and enough life experience to prove the lesson. In time, the Divine Child will be able to listen to his internal guidance and good council alike, and learn how to make the best choices for his life.

Eternal Child

**He approaches life with innocence.
He loves fun, play, and pleasure.**

Is this your child?

This archetype is fun. Wherever he goes, he will find a way to play. He enjoys physical activities that get him off the sofa and out into the world. Even when he grows up, he'll still be all for fun. He'll never outgrow his many friends, though they may outgrow him. He has a healthy, happy outlook on life and won't stay down for long. He has a charisma and charm that are contagious. It's easy to be a proud parent of such an enjoyable child. He'll definitely bring joy into your life—when you can keep up with him.

What brings out the best in this type?

The Eternal Child needs a place to spend his massive amounts of energy and zest for life. He'll do well in sports as long as the rules aren't too strict. He loves to have a busy schedule that includes interaction with people. He enjoys going to festivals and parties, and going on vacation.

How can this type be a challenge?

An Eternal Child may have a hard time sitting still and cause disturbances in the classroom; he can't be serious for very long. He can get completely lost in a game, losing track of time. Don't expect him to be home at a certain hour unless you call

Chapter 10: The Child Types

to remind him. He can lack a sense of responsibility so much you may wonder if he ever listens to you when you tell him his requirements. You may even wonder if he's being rebellious, because you gave such clear directions and he completely "forgot what you said."

When other kids are learning from their childish mistakes, he may keep making them and seem genuinely surprised by the repercussions. It takes him much longer to realize the inevitable consequences of his actions. With childlike enthusiasm, he'll just try it again; maybe this time he *can* flush a rock down the toilet.

As he matures into a teenager, he may be increasingly difficult to pin down. Showing up on time for family activities, remembering a birthday, or keeping his room even modestly clean can be a real challenge. Along with the natural freedoms that come with the teen years, it may seem like he's never where you expect him to be, and he's always surprised you're upset about it. He never means any harm; he was probably just having a nice time and forgot to call.

Okay, so now what do I do?

To parent an Eternal Child, find places to put his energy that won't cost you your energy. For example, the Eternal Child would do well in some sort of sport or frequent physical activity. Regular visits to a park or zoo will keep him entertained and happy. If he's a creative Eternal Child, it would be worth keeping a place for him to create that is always well stocked with paper, paints, and crayons.

Because these children are imaginative, it's helpful to hold on to their toys longer than other children. Having things for him to play with is better than trying to keep a neat house and then find him getting into things he shouldn't.

By far, the most challenging aspect of parenting this fun archetype is getting him to follow through with his responsibilities. The worst thing a parent can do is decide what is fair and appropriate, and just expect him to do it. The Eternal Child will resist responsibility more than most children, so it's futile to simply assume he'll follow the standard.

It would be much more efficient to try to turn cleaning into a fun game or allow the job to get done at a slower pace. Making up a game around picking up or completing tasks may seem like more effort, but for the Eternal Child it will actually make things easier and faster.

If a parent can't stop long enough to motivate the child, it may be better to just let him take his time. The Eternal Child may sit in his messy room and not move forward on cleaning for hours. If the parent can resist pressuring him but not let him out of doing the job, he'll eventually do his chores.

How to be with this type:

The key with this type is to give up expectations of how long the task will take. When a parent decides something like "When you clean your room you can go out and play," she must be willing to let him be stuck in that agreement until *he* completes it.

Every person in a family needs to pull their weight, but notice if you are feeling like you're spinning your wheels with this type. Are you constantly pushing him to follow through on tasks that aren't so much fun? Are you giving up making him do the boring jobs, knowing he's going to drag it on and on? Do you end up doing his work because it takes so long?

The Eternal Child will not spend eternity in his room refusing to clean it; he has to get out eventually. Use this as a tactic to stick to your decisions. If parents can leave him to his chores, homework, or practices, and let him decide when he wants to complete them so he can then have fun, the frustration will end. Eventually he'll realize the path to going out to play is faster if he just gets his chores done.

Wounded Child

**He is fiercely compassionate of
others who have suffered.**

Is this your child?

The Wounded Child is sensitive and compassionate. His ability to have empathy for others has come as a result of having experienced something that was very painful and difficult. The result of the trauma has left the child very sensitive to how others feel. Very young children may become needy or fearful in situations that remind them of the incident. The most important element that parents can take from this type is that these children have the capacity to nurture, heal, and help other people that are hurting.

What brings out the best in this type?

The Wounded Child has a tremendous capability to feel compassion. With this compassion he will want to help others to feel better. The Wounded Child is destined to help the world in some kind of healing way. His personal kind of healing will be reflective of how he was wounded.

For example, the child who has been injured in an accident will be the kind of person who encourages others to overcome physical challenges. The child who has recovered from a disease may become a medical professional or health advocate. Children who have been abused may become very protective

Family Types

of others. A child who has experienced some kind of deep wound will find it impossible to let someone else suffer as he did without trying to help.

How can this type be a challenge?

If your child has this type then the very fact that he was wounded is a hardship for parents. There will likely be guilt and sadness at the loss of innocence or normalcy. Just watching a child recover from any deep injury is challenging for parents. Parents should recognize that, even though something good can come from a terrible situation, we would never invite it in. As the parent of a Wounded Child, letting go of guilt may be a huge challenge.

At some point, after the wound has been addressed, a child with this type may have tendencies that have been shaped by his wound. Sometimes these tendencies turn negative, and it is helpful for parents to recognize them and help guide the child toward healthier responses.

For example, a child decides he has to try to save everyone from all their pain. This is irrational and too extreme to be healthy. While taking proactive steps to help others is a wonderful trait, the Wounded Child will take on too many "cases" and end up losing healthy boundaries and perspective.

A Wounded Child may try to help mend friendships, but in the end others turn their anger on him. Another possibility is that he may spend so much time helping others that he doesn't actually have fun himself. Children should not spend most of their time trying to fix others. Children who take on the worries of others to the detriment of their own dreams and desires need a parent to guide them in the wisdom of these choices.

Sometimes children take on their parents' worries as their own. Children who comfort parents are such a gift, but children

Chapter 10: The Child Types

will easily fall into the belief that it is their job to save their parents. If a child seems to be a worrier, and the worries are for other people, he will need guidance on how to find balance. Children lack adult perspective. A wise parent can make a huge difference in teaching that.

Okay, so now what do I do?

First, it's important to honor the gift of compassion that was born of the difficult situation. Acknowledge the beauty of his tender and nurturing spirit. Parents can thank the child if he is giving comfort. Then remind him that it's not his job to fix his parents. Although he can try to help them feel better, it's only if he really wants to. In other words, he's not obligated, but he is appreciated.

When a parent teaches that helping someone feel better is a gift and not an obligation, the child will learn to honor his capacity and not give too much. People who are too giving can go too far, get burned out, and become resentful because they haven't learned that it's not all their job.

If a Wounded Child has spent so much time and effort helping others, but has no friends of his own, he needs to learn how to develop his own healthy relationships. A Wounded Child may not realize that relationships are not for fixing, but for experiencing joy and companionship. While all long-term friendships contain issues that have to be dealt with, the majority of the time should be spent in experiencing companionship and fun. The Wounded Child may not have any idea that this is normal. He may not realize that sometimes just having fun and doing things together are what makes a happy life. Parents who spend time talking about this, and nudging their child toward simple, fun activities with others, will help the Wounded Child learn that fixing wounds doesn't have to be his full-time job.

Family Types

How to be with this type:

The gift of the Wounded Child is precious, and over time all of us benefit from his tender, compassionate heart. As parents of a Wounded Child we need to help him heal and create a life built on inspiration and joy. We can teach him about healthy relationships, where joy and companionship are most important. It's not necessary to accept the scars from a wound as inevitable. Although the Wounded Child will change and lose some of his innocence because of his experience, we can help him shape it into strength and compassion.

Orphan Child

**She is determined and destined to become independent.
She is outwardly self-assured.**

Is this your child?

The Orphan Child is not necessarily an actual orphan. Recognizing the pattern in a child doesn't mean her parents have been neglectful, either. The child with the Orphan type simply looks for others to be their parent.

The Orphan Child may have two perfectly normal parents, siblings, and a healthy family life, but she finds another family and acts like they are her second family. She may call her best friend's mother "Mom." She may have had the experience of spending a lot of time with a grandparent or other relative, and think of that person as her parent. The Orphan Child may or may not have issues at home, but she will look to the families of friends to give her guidance and comfort instead of looking to her own.

What brings out the best in this type?

The Orphan Child doesn't need deep roots at home because she can find a "home" with others. She's strong-willed and independent, and will desire to make her own way from the time she's little. Parents can rest assured knowing that, no matter how far she goes, she'll find close relationships that will fill her need for family. Although she won't seem to want or

Family Types

need her real family, in the end she's very family-focused and will create many strong bonds with others.

What brings out the worst in this type?

Sometimes the Orphan Child feels like the black sheep of the family. She may not feel that she fits in with the rest. From the perspective of the rest of the family, she may seem rebellious. Other family members may feel rejected because the Orphan Child looks to others as family.

The Orphan Child will often grow up and move away. If a family is close, it can be painful to "lose" a family member. Orphan Children often don't see the family they have right in front of them, because they just don't feel like they belong.

As an Orphan Child, it can be confusing to feel like a misfit. It's a sense of having been born into the wrong family, with no apparent reason. Dealing with those emotions can be disquieting. The Orphan Child may feel guilty if family members try to make sense of her preferences for other people, but can't.

Okay, so now what do I do?

Let her have her cake and eat it, too. As the parent of an Orphan Child it's important to realize you didn't cause this tendency, nor can you undo it. This child will think other people are as important as family members, and that can't be changed, but if parents can open up to accepting the influence of other people, they have a better shot at creating cooperation and understanding with their child. The kind of people the Orphan Child will choose to adopt will be the kind of people that take in "orphans." If parents can form a friendship with the chosen surrogate family, it will be easier to maintain healthy communication and influence over the child.

As the Orphan Child matures she will have a strong drive

Chapter 10: The Child Types

for independence and distance herself from her birth family. If the birth family helps her find healthy ways to feel independent, there will be less pull from the child. It may seem like parents are feeding a problem of desire for too much independence. Actually, that desire can't be tamed—only directed in the best possible direction.

For example, if an Orphan Child can get a job as a young teenager and make her own money, she'll feel more independent. If she can join a church group or other volunteer group, she may find "family connection" that could satisfy her needs.

How to be with this type:

The Orphan Child can be a challenge for families that are tight-knit. This type will do whatever it takes to branch out and form other close relationships. In the end, the more she is pressed into staying, the harder she'll work to leave. Keeping open arms and an understanding attitude will do more for helping maintain family bonds than anything else. If the Orphan Child feels free to come and go as early as possible, it will be easier for her to stay home.

For those children who have ended up feeling like they needed a new family and could not maintain a close relationship with their birth family, understanding this type may help soothe the feeling that they are missing out on a real family. Families are made many ways, and adopting new people into our lives is a positive and healthy response to our needs. It's a source of strength to be able to find and acclimate to new people. Our world is far from perfect. Creating new close relationships is one of the most powerful abilities for anyone.

Adult Child

He's extremely mature and responsible for his age.

Is this your child?

The Adult Child seems all grown up and is often in charge well before his time. He is either saddled with taking care of himself or others from a young age. He may be the firstborn in a house where the parents cannot be as available as needed. He may also take on the role of a missing parent.

What brings out the best in this type?

It is natural for him to take care of others, and make difficult and mature decisions. Usually he will be in charge of other children, and he's probably very good at it, too. He will make few mistakes, and likely embody a gentle and loving nature.

How can this type be a challenge?

He has a hard time relaxing and having fun. He's very serious about his responsibilities and feels more comfortable with grown-up type work than with play. He may become isolated from friends who are his own age. If a child has the Adult type he'll be more comfortable in charge, but he may need to have someone relieve him and get him to have fun more often.

Chapter 10: The Child Types

Okay, so now what do I do?

Although it seems cruel to put grown-up work on children, sometimes it's good for kids to learn responsibility. In fact, any time children can do something for themselves, they should. If one child has too much responsibility for others, and is not given time to just be a child, though, parents need to make sure that things become balanced. It's not enough to just take away some of his jobs either; he needs to have fun, too.

For example, parents need to help the Adult Child find things to do that are both stimulating and free from work. He will likely want to do more mature activities and may tire quickly of too much fun also. Even though play and games aren't natural or easy, it's worth the effort to help him learn to relax.

How to be with this type:

The Adult Child is easy to overlook because he seems to have it all together, but if you have this type in your family take the time to help him have some fun. These children don't realize that they are missing some important childhood experiences. Laughing, playing, and relaxing are parts of a healthy life, and even if he isn't natural with them, he needs to do them.

Acknowledgments

I want to share my deep gratitude to the following people, who were central in inspiring this book and guiding me thus far on my journey.

My husband Rob, you'll always be my Prince, and our three kids, the King, the Knight and the Warrior Princes, I'm so lucky to be your mom. Vincent and Inalyn Rose, my mom and dad, you two are a hard act to follow, but I'm trying. Cherith, Eden, Judea, and Tirzah, my four sisters who show how different, yet complimentary, family members can be. You each have inspired many pages of this book and always believe in me. My BFF Jana, and all the dear friends too numerous to list here, who have encouraged me along this path. Thank you all from the bottom of my heart.

Caroline Myss, you have been like a friend to me for well over a decade through your books, lectures, and classes. I thank you from the bottom of my heart for your fearless honesty. You have been a guiding light. This book is merely a synthesis of what I have learned from you.

The teachers and staff from CMED, particularly Lynn Bell and Peter Occhiogrosso. Your words still ring in my ears and throughout this book. And especially Jim Curtan, who has been like a kin spirit, showing me how each archetype is truly a gift.

To Coach Eva Gregory, thank you for keeping my focus clear and excitement high. Michael Katz, the Blue Penguin, for your help in shaping this book, which has made it the useful tool I hoped for. Cheryl Rogers, thank you for the great editing advice.

Finally, to all the children I have shared my life with, even those who are now grown, you gave me such perfect examples of each type. You have all taught me how wonderful every child can be when they are completely seen and understood.

About the Author

Selah Rose Cambias was a stay-at-home mother of three children when she decided to earn her Consulting Certificate from CMED (Caroline Myss Education Institute) in Chicago, Illinois. Selah had been studying *Sacred Contracts* by Caroline Myss for nearly a decade, and after returning from Chicago she realized her work with archetypes had begun to transform her relationships to her children. Selah started teaching others what she had been practicing, and in 2010 decided that parents could use a resource dedicated to understanding their children using archetypes. This book was created for that purpose.

Selah is now a family coach and helps parents develop a personalized parenting system based on their children's types.

For a free gift and more information on coaching, classes, and programs about the Family Types System™, please visit her website http://www.FamilyTypes.com.

www.ingramcontent.com/pod-product-compliance
Lightning Source LLC
LaVergne TN
LVHW051544070426
835507LV00021B/2396